Corporate Bonds and Commercial Paper

CORPORATE BONDS AND COMMERCIAL PAPER

Brian Coyle

FINANCIAL WORLD Publishing
THE CHARTERED INSTITUTE OF BANKERS

Financial World Publishing
IFS House
4-9 Burgate Lane
Canterbury
Kent
CT1 2XJ
United Kingdom

Telephone: 01227 818687

Financial World Publishing publications are published by
The Chartered Institute of Bankers, a non-profit-making registered educational charity.

Typeset by Kevin O'Connor
Printed in Italy

ISBN 0-85297-456-6

Contents

1

What are Corporate Bonds?

The term corporate bond is a general term for a negotiable long-term debt security issued by a company to raise capital and purchased by an investor. For example, a company wishing to raise $100 million of debt capital can do so by issuing bonds and selling them to investors.

Bonds Issued

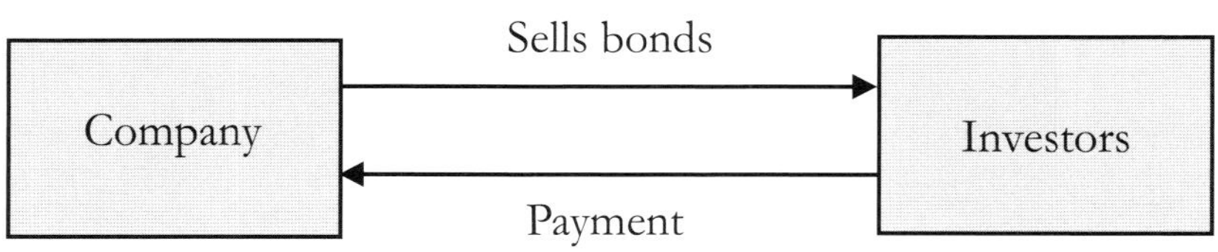

Bonds Redeemed at Maturity

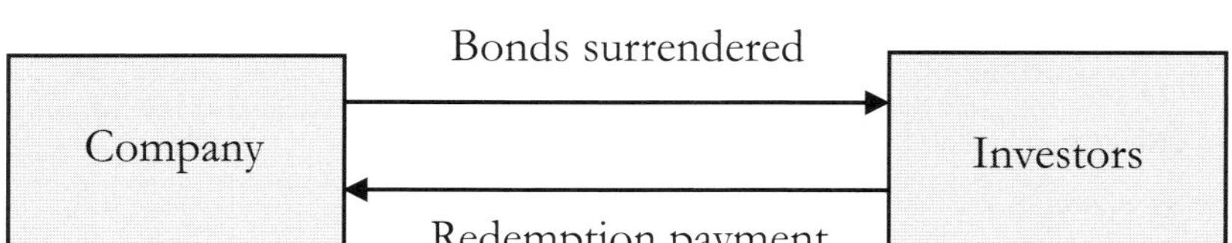

The bond issuer promises to repay the debt, a specified sum, to the bondholders at maturity either on a specified future date, or on any of a number of possible future dates, when the bonds will be redeemed for cash.

The purpose of issuing bonds is to raise long-term finance from the investment community as an alternative to borrowing from a bank. Investors are prepared to buy bonds to obtain the investment yield.

Nominal Value

Each bond has a fixed face value or nominal value. This is the amount that the company promises to repay at maturity if the debt is redeemable at par. However, the redemption value of bonds could be more than their nominal value (above par) depending on the specified terms of the bond issue.

While the price that investors pay for an issue of bonds is related to their nominal value, it is usually a higher or lower amount. A bond with a nominal value of $1,000 could be issued at a price of $1,000, but is more likely to be priced a bit lower or a bit higher, depending on:

- conditions in the bond market at the time of issue, and
- the rate of interest that investors will receive on the bond (the coupon) compared to the investment yield that investors expect to receive on similar bonds.

The reasons for having a nominal value for bonds are:

- to specify the amount of debt principal repayable at maturity. Debt is often redeemable at par. Even when a bond is redeemable above or below par, the redemption price is expressed relative to a par value of 100
- to specify the amount of interest payable on the bond until maturity. Interest is calculated on the nominal value of the bond.

Denominations

Normally bond certificates are issued in several denominations, for example as $1,000, $10,000, $100,000 and $1 million bonds. Differing denominations are selected to suit the requirements of investors. Small denominations generally are suitable for private retail investors and large denominations are preferred by institutional investors.

When bonds are issued in book entry (electronic) form, investors are required to apply for a minimum quantity of the bonds and in multiples of the minimum quantity, for example in a minimum quantity of $10,000 and in multiples of $10,000.

Coupons and Zero Coupons

Investors receive interest on their bonds. The method of earning interest differs between coupon bonds and zero coupon bonds or discount paper.

Coupon Bonds

For debt securities with a long term to maturity, it is usual to pay interest at regular intervals, typically every six or 12 months, but sometimes quarterly. The rate of interest is a percentage of the nominal value of the bond. This percentage rate is known as the coupon rate or coupon.

For example, 8% dollar-denominated bonds will pay interest of $8 per annum on each $100 nominal value of bonds. This could be paid in a single amount every year, but is more likely to be paid in six-monthly instalments of 4% each. Coupons usually are six-monthly for US and UK domestic corporate bonds, but annual for most eurobonds. Interest payment dates are specified when the bonds are issued and the payments are made on the issuer's behalf by an appointed paying agent, usually a bank.

Zero Coupon Bonds

Zero coupon bonds are bonds that are redeemable at par at maturity, but pay no coupon rate of interest. Short-term zero-coupon debt securities are known as discount paper, and include commercial paper.

Zero coupon bonds are issued at a discounted price to their nominal value. Investors make their return (profit) from the difference between the issue price of the bonds and their eventual redemption price. This return is, in effect, the accumulated interest on their investment, and can be expressed as an annual rate of interest on the investment.

For example, five-year zero coupon bonds paying interest annually and issued at a price of 70.00, $70 for each $100 nominal value of bonds, would provide the purchaser with a yield of about 7½% per annum between issue date and redemption. If a holder of these zero coupon bonds wished to sell the investment before their redemption date, the price obtainable in the secondary bond market would depend on bond yields at the time of the sale, but it would be above 70.00. The difference between the sale price and the original purchase price would represent the bondholder's return on investment.

Calculating Interest

There are different methods of calculating the interest payable on coupon bonds. These various methods are known as interest-rate conventions, and a different convention applies to bonds in different bond markets. The interest-rate conventions differ, for example, between US corporate bonds, UK corporate bonds and most eurobonds.

An investor should make sure that he/she knows which convention applies to any particular bond issue.

- Actual/360 day convention. The interest payable on the bonds in any interest-rate period is calculated as follows:

$$\text{Nominal value} \times \text{Annual coupon (\%)} \times \frac{\text{Actual days in period}}{360}$$

- Actual/365 day convention. The interest payable on the bonds in any interest-rate period is calculated as follows:

$$\text{Nominal value} \times \text{Annual coupon (\%)} \times \frac{\text{Actual days in period}}{365}$$

- 30/360 day convention. This convention assumes every month has 30 days, and a year consists of 360 days. The interest payable on the bonds in any interest-rate period is calculated as follows:

$$\text{Nominal value} \times \text{Annual coupon (\%)} \times \frac{\text{(Actual months in period} \times 30)}{360}$$

- Actual/Actual convention (ISMA definition). This might appear to mean that interest is calculated on the basis of the actual number of days in the interest period divided by the actual number of days in the year. Oddly, this is not necessarily the case, and there are different definitions of what Actual/Actual means. The ISMA definition that has applied to euro-denominated eurobonds since January 1999, is as follows.

$$\text{Nominal value} \times \text{Annual coupon (\%)} \times \frac{\text{Calendar days in period}}{\text{(Calendar days in period)} \times \text{(Number of interest periods in the year)}}$$

Example
Some 7% bonds pay interest six-monthly, and the interest periods are 20 January to 19 July, and 20 July to 19 January. These are interest periods of 181 days and 184 days respectively.

- If an Actual/360-day convention applies, interest in each six-month period each year would be, for each $1,000 of bonds, ($1,000 x 7% x 181/360) and ($1,000 x 7% x 184/360), i.e. $35.19 and $35.78 respectively.
- If an Actual/365-day convention applies, interest in each six-month period each year would be, for each $1,000 of bonds, ($1,000 x 7% x 181/365) and ($1,000 x 7% x 184/365), i.e. $34.71 and $35.29 respectively.
- If a 30/360-day convention applies, interest in each six-month period each year would be, for each $1,000 of bonds, ($1,000 x 7% x (6 x 30)/360), i.e. $35.00.
- If an Actual/Actual convention (ISMA definition) applies,

interest in each six-month period would be, for each $1,000 of bonds, ($1,000 x 7% x 181/(181 x 2)) and ($1,000 x 7% x 184/(184 x 2)), i.e. $35 in each period.

US corporate bonds pay interest on an Actual/360-day basis. Sterling bonds pay interest on an Actual/365-day basis, and many eurobonds and some US bonds pay interest on a 30/360-day basis.

Fixed and Floating-Rate Interest

Coupon bonds pay interest at either a fixed or floating-rate (variable-rate) of interest.

The rate of interest for fixed coupons is expressed as a percentage of the nominal value of the bonds, and remains the same until maturity. Fixed coupon debt securities without any additional features, such as call options or put options, also are referred to as straight debt or plain vanilla debt.

Bonds that pay interest at a variable rate are called floating-rate notes or FRNs. The coupon-rate of interest is set at a spread or margin above a reference or benchmark rate. This is a readily identifiable market interest rate. For sterling bonds, it is usually the six-month London Interbank Offered Rate (LIBOR) when interest is paid six-monthly. For euro-denominated bonds, the benchmark may be the EBF euribor rate, and for dollar-denominated eurobonds the usual benchmark is the dollar LIBOR rate.

For example, interest on FRNs might be 12.5 basis points above six-month LIBOR. One basis point is 0.01%, and 100 basis points represent 1%. When the rate of interest is 12.5 basis points above six-month LIBOR, the interest rate payable in a given interest period will be one-eighth of one per cent above the six-month LIBOR rate, and the LIBOR rate will be obtained by reference to a published LIBOR rate at a particular time of day, typically on the day before the beginning of the interest period in question. Therefore, the interest payable on FRNs in each interest period is known at the start of the interest period, and paid at the end of the period.

The rate of interest payable varies from one payment date to the next because of changes in the reference or benchmark rate of interest. The rate payable for the next interest period is reset on a fixing date or rollover date by adding the spread or margin to whatever the reference rate of interest happens to be on the reset date.

Example
Alpha plc has two types of sterling-denominated bond in issue.

- 7% loan stock 2012, on which interest is payable six-monthly, on June 5 and December 5.
- Floating Rate Notes 2007, on which interest is payable six-monthly, on April 17 and October 17. The rate of interest payable is 50 basis points (0.50%) over six-month LIBOR. For payments on April 17, the interest rate is reset by reference to six-month LIBOR at 12 a.m. on the preceding October 17. For payments on October 17, the interest rate is reset by reference to six-month LIBOR at 12 a.m. on the preceding April 17.

Analysis
On the fixed coupon loan stock, the company will pay interest of 7% per annum per £100 nominal value of the stock on June 5 and December 5 each year until maturity in June or December in 2002, applying the appropriate interest-rate convention.

On the FRNs, the rate of interest varies with changes in LIBOR. If the market rate for LIBOR on April 17 2005 were 7.00% per annum, interest would be paid on the FRNs on the October 17 2005 at a rate of 7.50% per annum (7.00% + the spread of 0.50%) for that particular period, applying the appropriate interest-rate convention to the calculation..

An agent bank for the bond issuer will announce the interest rate for the next interest rate period in a newspaper advertisement. An example is shown opposite.

Alpha Beta Corporation Finance BV

$100,000,000
Floating rate subordinated notes due July 2015

> In accordance with the provisions of the notes, notice is hereby give that for the interest period 19 January 2002 to 19 July 2002 the notes will carry an interest rate of 5.875% per annum. Interest payable on the relevant interest payment date 19 July 2002 will amount to $259.383 per denomination of $10,000 note.

Agent: Omega Bank

Date of announcement January 19 2002

FRNs with Embedded Floors
A drawback to FRNs, from an investor's point of view, is that market interest rates could fall, and the interest paid on the FRNs could drop below an acceptable level. Therefore FRNs are sometimes issued with an embedded floor that is a guarantee of a minimum rate of interest. These also are known as drop-lock FRNs.

Example
FRNs could be issued offering interest at the six-month LIBOR rate minus 25 basis points (0.25%), with an embedded floor of 6%. If six-month LIBOR remains at 6.25% or over, the FRNs will pay LIBOR minus 25 basis points. However, if six-month LIBOR falls below 6.25%, the interest on the FRNs will be 6%, the floor rate of interest.

Collared FRNs
A collared floating-rate note is a bond issue paying a variable rate of interest, subject to both a maximum and a minimum rate of interest. For example, a company might make a $100-million ten-year issue of FRNs, for which the interest rate is six-month LIBOR minus 25 basis points, subject to a minimum rate of 5.125% and a maximum rate of 8.25%.

Maturities

The maturity of a debt security is the period of time to redemption. Maturities can be expressed either:

- according to the term to redemption at the time of their issue, or
- according to the remaining time to redemption, for securities already in issue.

Example
Suppose a bond was issued in 1996 with a redemption date in the year 2001.

The original maturity of the bond was 15 years (from 1996 to 2011). However, if the current year were 2003, the current maturity of the bond would be eight years.

Bonds, Notes and Commercial Paper

A major distinction between bonds, notes and commercial paper is their original maturity, as at the date of issue.

- Bonds are long-term debt securities with an original maturity of seven years or longer.
- Notes are medium-term debt securities with an original maturity of about two to seven years. However, with the development of the medium-term notes market, maturities of notes can be shorter than two years and longer than seven years. This is explained in Chapter 7.
- Commercial paper or CP is short-term corporate debt with an original maturity of up to nine months or one year.

Short, Intermediate and Long Coupons
Securities with a short remaining term to maturity (up to two years) are referred to as short coupons. With a remaining maturity of two to seven

years they are called intermediate coupons. Bonds with over seven years remaining to maturity are called long coupons.

Redemption

A bond or note or CP is redeemed when the issuer repays the principal amount of the debt to the bondholder at maturity. Most bonds are redeemed by a single lump-sum payment at maturity. This is known as bullet redemption, and is similar in concept to a bullet repayment of a bank loan.

Some bond issues provide for early redemption, before maturity, at the choice of either:

- the bondholder who is given a put option, or
- the issuer who has a call option.

Put Options

Bonds can be issued with a put option. This gives bondholders the right, if they wish to exercise it, to ask for early redemption of their bonds. The payment on redemption may be at at a discount to nominal value, i.e. at a price below par.

The purpose of a put option with a fixed-coupon bond could be to make the bond issue more attractive to investors. If market interest rates rise above the fixed rate payable on the bonds, the bondholders can exercise their put option, redeem the bonds and use the money to invest in new bonds yielding a higher rate of interest. Therefore put options give protection to bondholders against the risk of a rise in market interest rates.

Example

Beta, a multinational company, issues 5% ten-year bonds. The bonds have a put option, giving their holders the right at any time from three years after the issue date, to redeem their bonds early. Beta wants use of all the funds for at least three years, and so the put option is not exercisable before that time.

Analysis

Investors will buy the bonds to receive a fixed rate of interest at 5%. However, market rates of interest could rise after the issue has been made, and the rate of interest on new issues of similar bonds could be 8% for example. Investors receiving 5% on Beta's bonds could feel that they have lost out because, by investing in Beta, they cannot put their money into 8% bonds.

The put option, however, allows the bondholders to oblige Beta to redeem their bonds so that they can switch to investing in higher-yielding bonds.

Put Options and Restructuring Events

Bondholders also might be able to exercise a put option if a restructuring event occurs in the business of the bond issuer. A restructuring event might be a change of control of the bond issuer, or a major asset disposal by the bond issuer. Bondholders might be allowed to redeem their bonds at par or a price close to par, as soon as such an event occurs.

An example of the potential problem of a restructuring event arose in the sterling bond market during 2000. Newly demerged company Thorn made a £100 million bond issue. The bond did not have a change-of-control put option for bondholders. Thorn was acquired by Nomura soon after the issue and subsequently was loaded up with debt, and many of the company's assets were securitized. As a result, the Thorn bonds became almost untradable. The Thorn experience prompted banks specializing in the sterling bond market to insist that new bond issues should include a put option giving bondholders the right to redeem their bonds at par in the event of a change of control.

Call Options

A call option with a bond issue gives the issuer the right, if it so wishes, to redeem the bonds before their specified maturity date, by giving notification, typically 30 or 60 days, to the bondholders. Such bonds are known as callable bonds.

Whereas put options protect investors against rising market interest rates, call options protect the issuer of fixed-coupon bonds against a fall in interest rates.

When a fixed-rate bond is issued with a call option and market interest rates then fall, the issuer can redeem the issue early. It can then refinance its funding requirements by making a new bond issue at a lower coupon rate of interest.

Example
A company issues £100 million of 8% callable bonds. Subsequently interest rates fall so that a similar bond issue could now be made at 6%.

Analysis
The company could call in the bonds and refinance its borrowing requirement by making a new issue of £100 million 6% bonds with the same maturity. This would save the company 200 basis points on the cost of its borrowing, i.e. £2 million each year in interest payments.

Call Protection
Bonds with a call option give protection to the issuer of the bonds at the expense of the investors. For example, if bonds were issued at a fixed rate of 10%, and interest rates fell, a 10% coupon rate will become a very attractive investment. A call option on the bonds could deprive the bondholder of this above-average coupon rate if the bond issuer were to insist on early redemption.

To give investors some protection against this sort of action by the issuer, it is usual for bond issues to include some call protection for investors.

- An issue could be non-callable. The issuer would be prevented from calling in or redeeming the issue before maturity.

- An issue with a call option could be non-callable for the first few years after issue.
- An issue could be callable, except in a situation where the issuer wishes to call in the issue and seek replacement funds from a cheaper new issue. These bonds are referred to as callable except for refunding purposes.

If bonds are callable, the call option most often will provide for early redemption at a premium. For example, if an issuer of bonds wished to redeem them early, the redemption price could be 102 ($102 per $100 face value of the bonds). The size of this early redemption premium should diminish over time as the issue approaches maturity.

Perpetual Bonds

Some bonds have no redemption date and are irredeemable. The bondholders receive interest every year in perpetuity. These bonds are known as perpetuals.

Sinking Funds

A bond issuer is sometimes required to make annual cash payments into a fund. The cash is invested, and the accumulated fund, known as a sinking fund, can be spent on redeeming bonds in the issue. The fund is administered by an independent manager, a trustee in the US or UK, who is responsible for investing the cash paid into the fund, and for using money in the accumulated fund to redeem bonds in the market from bondholders who are willing to sell.

Debt Certificates and Book-Entry Systems

Bonds and notes might be issued in paper form as a certificate. The certificate shows an acknowledgement of the debt by the issuer, and the bondholder's rights, e.g. to payment of interest on specific dates through a named paying agent. However, there are several drawbacks to using certificates including:

- the cost of producing them
- in some cases, the administrative work required for any transfer of ownership
- in the case of bearer bonds, the risk of losing certificates.

Paper-based systems of ownership and transfer can be cumbersome so book-entry systems have been developed that are operated by central securities depositories. In a book-entry system, ownership is recorded in a computerized stock account for the investor. Transfers of ownership also are made by means of a computer entry, eliminating the need for a certificate to change hands. The system also will provide for the payment for the bonds to be made by the purchaser against transfer of ownership of the bond.

Registered Bonds and Bearer Bonds

Certificates are issued in either:

- registered form, or
- bearer form.

The issuer keeps a record or register of the owners of registered bonds and notes. Transfers of ownership must be notified and recorded in the register. Interest payments are mailed to the registered owner.

Physical possession of the certificate is proof of ownership of bearer bonds and notes. The issuer does not know the identity of the bondholders. The bond or note carries tear-off coupons, one for each interest payment date. When interest payments are due, the owner submits a tear-off interest coupon and gives it to the issuer's paying agent who will make the payment as directed. At maturity, bearer bonds are redeemed by sending in the certificate for repayment.

Because physical possession of bearer bonds is evidence of ownership, it is important for investors to provide for their safekeeping. Consequently, bearer securities usually are lodged with a bank, custodian or central securities depository. This organization also will arrange for interest payments to be collected on each interest-payment date.

When bonds are held in book-entry form, interest payments are made through the central securities depository.

Secured and Unsecured Debt

Debt securities can be either secured or unsecured. Security is provided in the form of a charge on specified assets of the business. In the event of the issuer failing to make a scheduled payment of interest, or loan principal, secured bondholders can seek repayment from the proceeds of selling off the charged assets. In the US or UK, bondholders, through their trustee, would appoint a receiver with the task of selling the assets on their behalf. Unsecured bondholders rank with other creditors in order of priority for payment but in the case of subordinated debt, bondholders rank *below* other creditors in priority for payment.

Seniority of Debt

Debt securities can be ranked by seniority according to the entitlement of the security holders to payment in an event of default and liquidation of the borrower's business.

- Senior debt consists of secured loans that rank ahead of other creditors, to the extent that the loan is covered by the value of the security.
- Debenture stock is secured loan stock that has a charge on the assets of the business. If debenture stock is not senior debt, it will have a second charge over the assets of the business, and so would rank behind senior debt.

- Junior debt is unsecured loan stock that ranks with other unsecured creditors in a liquidation.
- A subordinated loan is an unsecured loan that usually ranks behind other unsecured creditors in a liquidation.

Covenants

Corporate bonds are not risk-free so bond investors might require some protection against the credit risk in the form of covenants, and a bond issue might have covenants attached. A covenant is an undertaking by the borrower, written into the documentation for the debt issue, to comply with a specified condition. Compliance with covenants is monitored, and breach of a covenant constitutes an event of default, giving the bondholders the right to demand accelerated repayment, i.e. immediate redemption of their bonds. Covenants are given for bank loans as well as for bonds, but usually are more stringent with loans than with bonds.

Trustee

A company wishing to issue bonds in the US or UK must decide whether or not to use a trustee. (Other European countries do not recognize the legal concept of trustee, but to obtain an official listing and be accepted for trading on the London Stock Exchange, a bond issued by a UK company must have a trustee.)

The role of the trustee is to:

- enter the loan agreement/trust deed with the borrower on behalf of the lenders/investors
- hold any security on behalf of the lenders/investors
- monitor compliance by the borrower with the loan agreement/trust deed, including covenants
- take action in an event of default, e.g. call for accelerated repayment

- act as a channel for discussion between the borrower and investors.

Governing Law

Every bond issue must be subject to the law and jurisdiction of a particular country. This is the law and the judicial procedures that will be used to resolve any dispute between the issuer and the bondholders. The choice of governing law for a debt program can be critical. When an issuer has two or more debt programs, each subject to a different governing law, the terms of the issue, e.g. the meaning of covenants, could be interpreted differently. The governing law should be one that offers reasonable protection to both the bond issuer and investors in each country.

Conclusion

Corporate debt securities are a means whereby companies can obtain funding from investors. They vary in form and structure in maturity, interest-rate basis, in the nature of security and covenants, to suit the requirements of both borrowers and investors.

Securities can be issued in any of several debt markets. The features of the debt markets are the subject of the next chapter.

2

The Debt Markets

The debt markets exist for issuing and investing in debt securities. This chapter explains the general features of the markets.

Market Participants

There are three main groups of participants in the debt markets:

- issuers
- investors, and
- intermediaries.

Issuers

Issuers of debt securities use the markets to raise capital and consist mainly of:

- governments and supranational organizations, and
- financial, commercial and industrial companies.

Central governments (sovereign issuers) are major borrowers in the markets. They have a very strong influence on the corporate debt markets for two reasons.

- Interest rates on corporate bonds might be set by reference to interest rates on government bonds with the same maturity at a spread above the government borrowing rate.
- Heavy borrowing in the markets by a central government can squeeze corporate issuers out of the market. Investors have a finite amount of money to invest, but when a government is

forced to borrow heavily, it will pay whatever interest is necessary to attract enough buyers. As a result borrowing by companies could become excessively expensive.

Supranational organizations such as the World Bank and European Investment Bank (EIB) also are large borrowers in the markets. They have a top-quality credit rating because their borrowings are guaranteed by central governments or the United Nations in the case of the World Bank or the European Community nations in the case of the EIB. Supranationals use the debt markets in the same way as companies.

Companies that borrow in the debt markets can be classified as banks and similar financial institutions, and non-bank corporates, i.e. non-bank commercial and industrial companies. However, both banks and corporates use the corporate debt markets in the same way to raise funds. The main distinction between them is the purpose for which capital is being raised. Banks borrow to relend and to provide other financial services, whereas corporates can be regarded as the end users of capital.

It is also quite usual for a large global company to establish a special finance subsidiary that raises debt finance on behalf of the parent company and the rest of the group. For example, a global company, the Epsilon Corporation, might have a Dutch-based finance subsidiary, Epsilon Corporation Finance BV. If the group wants to raise capital, the finance subsidiary might issue bonds in its own name, but its payment of interest to bondholdes and the redemption of the bond principal at maturity will be guaranteed by Epsilon Corporation, the parent company, and possibly also by some of the other subsidiary companies in the Epsilon group.

Investors

The debt markets in most countries are dominated by domestic and foreign institutional investors. The main investing institutions vary from country to country, depending on the national financial framework. In general they consist of insurance and life assurance companies, investment companies, pension funds, unit trust funds or mutual funds, and possibly banks.

There are also private investors. In the earlier years of the eurobond markets, wealthy individuals were major investors. This is because eurobonds can have two major attractions for private investors.

- Because they are bearer bonds, and their owners could deposit them with a cross-border bank, perhaps in Luxembourg. The investors could keep their identity hidden, the bank acting as their agent in collecting interest.
- Interest on eurobonds is paid gross, without the issuer deducting any taxes, so individuals could evade tax by investing in eurobonds.

Eurobond dealers sometimes refer descriptively to small retail investors as Belgian dentists who buy eurobonds across the border in Luxembourg and deposit the bonds with a Luxembourg bank. Private investors still use the eurobond markets, but the main investors in bonds are now institutional buyers.

Intermediaries

Intermediaries in the markets act as a go-between for issuers and investors to make the markets function efficiently. The main activities of capital markets intermediaries are:

- origination – bringing a new issue to the market
- syndication and underwriting – guaranteeing funds to the issuer
- distribution – selling an issue, and
- secondary market trading – making a market

Often within each market, there will be a small number of major intermediaries that handle a large proportion of the total volume of transactions. For example, in the eurobond market a large proportion of activity is handled by a fairly small number of securities house and investment banks. The role of intermediaries in the securities markets is to bring together issuers and investors, rather than to invest their own funds in securities.

Domestic and International Markets (Euromarkets)

The markets for bonds, notes and commercial paper can be classified as either domestic or international.

Domestic Markets

Domestic capital markets were developed to enable issuers to raise capital, primarily from investors in their own country. Domestic markets are now much more international in character, and are used by foreign as well as domestic issuers and investors. The main features of a domestic market are:

- it is subject to the laws of a single national government, and
- it is regulated by a national organization.

The London Stock Exchange, for example, is a domestic market in the UK, governed by UK law. Members of the exchange are subject to regulation by a government agency, the Financial Services Authority (FSA), and the exchange may operate only because it has been granted recognition as an investment exchange by the FSA.

International Bond Markets

The international capital markets (or euromarkets) originated from the growth of off-shore funds in major traded currencies, particularly dollars. Offshore funds are funds held in another country, for example funds held in a bank in Switzerland by a US company. Many offshore funds are in eurocurrencies, particularly eurodollars. A eurocurrency is a deposit held with a bank outside the currency's country or origin. For example, eurodollars are dollars held in an account with a bank outside the US. These funds can be used by the deposit-taking banks for relending, or can be invested by their owners.

The international markets are referred to as the euromarkets. Although operating mainly in European countries, they are not restricted to Europe. Three euromarkets might be distinguished, those for:

- bonds (eurobonds)
- medium-term notes (euroMTNs), and
- commercial paper (eurocommercial paper or ECP).

The main features of a euromarket are:

- securities are issued simultaneously and subsequently traded in more than one country
- dealers within each country are subject to the laws of their country, but the market as a whole is not subject to the regulation of any single national government or statutory authority.

The international market is self-regulated, with rules for such activities as issuing and trading securities established by a voluntary association of market dealers. In the eurobond market, for example, bonds are issued and traded by syndicates of dealers in several countries. The dealers acting as intermediaries are subject to the laws of the country in which they operate. However, rules governing practise within the market have been established by two self-regulatory bodies:

- the International Primary Markets Association (IPMA) for new bond issues, and
- the International Securities Market Association (ISMA), for the secondary international bond markets.

Domestic Bonds and Foreign Bonds

Bonds issued in a domestic market can be either domestic or foreign. Domestic bonds are issued by a domestic company or institution, i.e. one from the country in which the market is located. Foreign bonds are issued in a domestic market by an issuer from another country. The issuer can be either a foreign government or a foreign company, including a multinational based in another country.

Foreign bonds are given a variety of names, for example:

- yankee bonds – bonds issued in the US by a non-US organization

- bulldog bonds – bonds issued in the UK by a non-UK organization
- samurai bonds – bonds issued in the Japan by a non-Japanese organization
- matador bonds – bonds issued in Spain by a non-Spanish organization

The Debt Markets

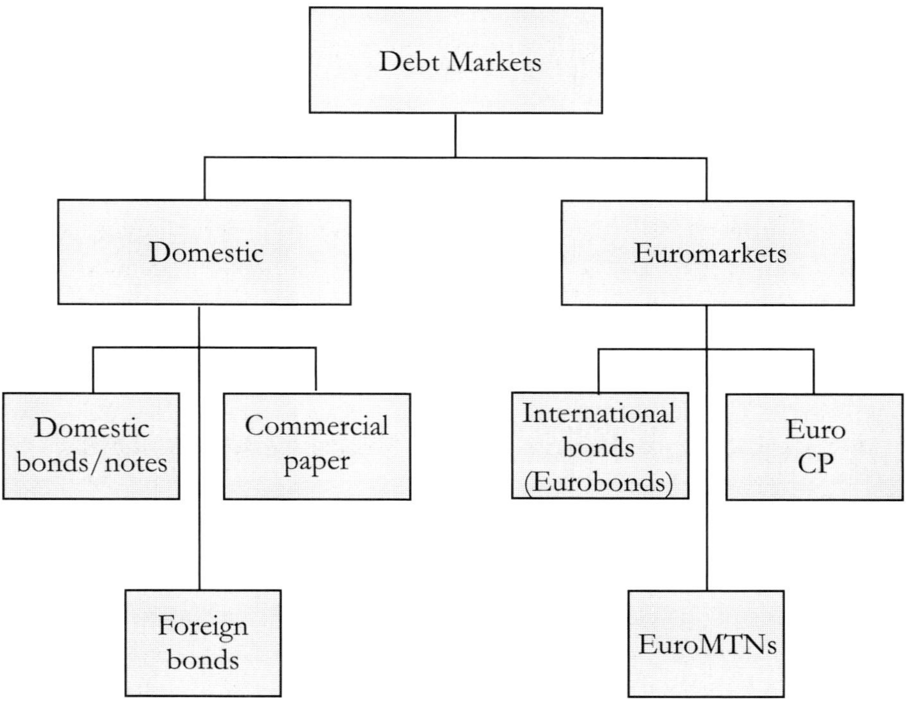

High-Yield Bonds (Junk Bonds)

A section of the US domestic bond market and the international bond market is classified as a high-yield-bond market or junk-bond market. Junk bonds refer to bond issues that have a credit rating in a category below investment-grade status. As a result, investors in the bonds demand a higher yield to compensate them for the high credit risk.

The junk bond market is much larger and better developed than the high-yield bond market in Europe. Investors in junk bonds in Europe tend to buy and hold the bonds in order to enjoy the high interest income, and as a consequence the junk bond market in Europe is fairly illiquid.

Identification Numbers for Bond Issues

Given the large number of different bond issues, and the computerization of much bond ownership, it is perhaps unsurprising that systems of identification numbers have been developed for bond issues.

- Each issue of securities is given a unique code number, known as its International Securities Identification Number or ISIN.
- In the US, bond issues are given a CUSIP number. CUSIP stands for Committee on Uniform Securities Identification Procedures. Government bonds as well as corporate and municipal bonds are given a CUSIP number. These are assigned, for the payment of a fee, by Standard & Poor's.

Global Markets

A global issue is an issue of securities in more than one market at the same time. For example, an issue of dollar bonds in both the US domestic market and the eurobond market would be a global issue. In subsequent secondary-market trading, the bonds could be traded between the markets, thereby creating a global market.

Primary Markets and Secondary Markets

A distinction is made between primary and secondary capital markets.

- Primary markets are for the issue of new securities to raise capital. They bring together issuers and investors who are invited to purchase the new securities, typically at a fixed-issue price.
- Secondary markets are for the subsequent trading of securities between investors, and also can be used by issuers to redeem debt early, before maturity.

A secondary market can be provided by a stock exchange. Companies issuing new securities can apply to have them officially listed, and admitted to trading on a stock exchange. If they are accepted into listing and admitted to trading, the securities can be traded on the exchange.

Most secondary-market trading in bonds is not conducted through an exchange but over-the-counter or through an electronic bond-trading platform. The key to successful secondary bond trading is liquidity and volume of trading. There should be enough dealers willing to act as intermediaries between investors for selling and buying. Even within an over-the-counter market, there has to be some accepted procedures for trading, for example for quoting prices and confirming and settling transactions. A system for trading international bonds in the secondary bond market, and an electronic system for dealing, is provided by ISMA.

A secondary capital market does not raise any new capital for the bond issuer, but does give investors an opportunity to trade investments in their portfolios. By selling securities they can realize a capital gain or loss on their investments. The secondary market also gives them the option of buying securities already in issue, as an alternative to buying new issues in the primary market. This provides them with a wider choice of investment opportunities.

E Bonds

The term E bonds refers to bonds that are issued by means of an offer to the public over the internet. Trading platforms are being developed to facilitate this type of issue and secondary market trading. To date, only a small number of such issues have been made.

Market Liquidity

An active or liquid secondary market is often essential to attract investors. A liquid market is one in which investors can sell or buy securities readily at a fair price. Unless the secondary market is likely to be liquid, many investors will avoid the primary market, and will not put money into new issues. Issuers, although not directly involved in the secondary markets, therefore must be concerned about secondary market liquidity.

Liquidity varies between markets and over time. For example, at a given time, the eurobond markets might be liquid for bonds denominated in dollars, yen and euros, but less liquid for bonds denominated in other currencies such as sterling or the Canadian dollar. At another time, the eurobond market might be illiquid for yen-denominated bonds, but more liquid for sterling bonds.

The domestic bond markets in the US are fairly liquid, whereas the UK domestic bond market has a much lower level of secondary-market trading. Domestic bond issues in the UK therefore are fairly infrequent.

A key function of intermediaries is to stimulate secondary-market activity by making a market in the securities, so dealers acting as lead managers for bond issues will make a market in the bonds. They also can encourage other intermediaries to make a secondary market. This is particularly important in the eurobond market, where secondary-market trading should be available in several international financial centers.

Public Offerings and Private Placements

There are two ways in which a new issue of securities can be distributed to investors:

- by a public offering, sometimes called an initial public offering or IPO, and
- through a private placement or placing.

In a public offering, the securities are offered to the general investing public through a stock exchange. For an issuer the main advantage of a public offering is the ability to sell securities to a large target market of investors that could be necessary to raise a large amount of capital.

In a private placement, the securities are marketed, usually by a group of selling banks acting for the bond issuer, to selected investment institutions. A private placement can be used for issuing securities within the regulations of a stock exchange. Private placements are cheaper and involve less documentation than a public offering. In the eurobond markets, all issues are privately placed.

Exchange Markets and Private Placement Markets

In an exchange market, bonds are traded through a stock exchange.

- If a primary issue is made by initial public offering, the general public will be invited to subscribe for the bonds through dealers on the exchange and in accordance with exchange procedures.
- If a primary issue is made by private placement, the exchange usually will require some bonds in the issue to be set aside for offering to the general public.

When bonds are listed on an exchange, they can be traded through exchange dealers in the secondary market. It is quite common, however, for private transactions to be arranged directly between investors, or using an electronic trading platform, without using a stock-exchange dealer as intermediary.

A private-placement market is a market for securities issued originally by private placement. There might be government restrictions on trading in unlisted securities, and these can prevent a private-placement market from developing. In the US, however, a relaxation of the rules for trading in unlisted securities in 1990 resulted in the expansion of a fairly liquid private-placement market. This is sometimes referred to as the Rule 144A market.

The secondary market in eurobonds is organized by securities dealers.

Typically, the bank that acted as the lead manager of the original bond issue, together with some other banks, might undertake to create a secondary market in the specific bond issues.

Gray Market

The gray market describes trading in a new issue of securities before the issue actually takes place. Transactions between sellers and buyers are arranged for future settlement after the issue. The gray market also is referred to as the when-issued (WI) market. The sellers of securities in a gray market are selling short because they will have to buy securities when they are eventually issued in order to settle.

An advantage of the gray market for bond issues is that the issuer can assess market conditions up to the time of the issue before deciding what the issue price should be.

A gray market for eurobonds has operated for several years, and since 1988 has been permitted by the London Stock Exchange for domestic issues of fixed-interest securities.

Clearing and Settlement

Clearing is the process by which the details of a transaction for buying and selling securities are agreed formally between the parties, and arrangements are made for settlement.

Once a transaction has been agreed between dealers for the seller and the buyer, the details have to be checked and confirmed. This is to make sure that both parties have understood each other properly, and agree the details. One error, not as unusual as it should be, is for both parties to think they are selling, or both to think they are buying the investments in question. There also could be important misunderstandings about the quantity and price of the securities being traded.

The procedures by which the details of a transaction are confirmed vary, but the normal principle is that:

- each party inputs the details of the transaction into a system for processing, and
- the details input by each party are matched and confirmed.

In an electronic trading system, trade input and matching are carried out within the system. When deals are made by telephone, the dealers input the trade details into their own internal system, and matching and confirmation are carried out by an exchange of fax messages.

Settlement is the process whereby securities are delivered to the buyer on the settlement date for the transaction, normally a few days after the transaction date, and the buyer pays for them. When settlement is delivery versus payment, the delivery of the securities to the buyer and the payment for them take place at the same time.

Depositories

Most institutional investors do not want the administrative burden of:

- accepting delivery of investments they have bought
- looking after them
- making sure that interest payments are made on time
- arranging the transfer of funds to pay for securities they have bought.

Specialist organizations exist to do this administrative work for them. These organizations may be either depositories or custodians.

In the eurobond market, the task of safeguarding the securities of investors and administering them is carried out by two international securities depositories or ISDs:

- Euroclear, and
- Clearstream.

The functions of Euroclear and Clearstream include:

- providing a system for settlement of transactions in securities on behalf of their participants, including transactions in eurobonds, and
- a book-entry system for holding bonds in dematerialized form by means of electronic stock accounts.

Participants in either Euroclear or Clearstream hold two accounts with the organization:

- a securities clearance account that maintains a record of the securities they hold within the system and in what quantities, and
- a cash account.

When a participant buys securities:

- the securities are added to his/her securities clearance account on settlement date, and
- the payment is made out of his/her cash account.

Similarly, when a participant sells securities:

- the securities are taken out of his/her securities clearance account on settlement date, and
- a payment is made into his/her cash account.

The physical bond certificates, or the legal instrument for the bond issue, do not have to move.

The depositories also handle interest payments and payments of principal on redemption on behalf of the client by submitting the interest-payment coupons or, on redemption, the certificates for payment. Interest on the bonds is paid into the participant's cash account. This service saves the owners of the bonds the administrative task of having to do the work themselves. The depositories are able to handle interest payments in bulk for a number of investors at the same time, thereby saving effort and expense.

Euroclear and Clearstream also provide for trading between themselves, and each has a securities account and cash account with the other. This electronic trading link is known as the bridge. By means of the bridge, a participant in Clearstream can make a transaction with a participant in Euroclear, and the transaction can be processed by book entry within the two systems. Again, there is no requirement for a physical movement of the bond certificates. This link between the organizations is important because it means an investment institution participating in either organization will be able to settle transactions in eurobonds with every other major investment or financial institution in the international markets.

The Depository Trust and Clearing Corporation (DTCC)

In the US a similar function is carried out by the Depository Trust and Clearing Corporation (DTCC). The DTCC offers a broader range of services, however, including:

- acting as central counterparty to market transactions
- acting as a netting agent in the financial markets.

A central counterparty is an organization representing the market exchange on which a transaction in securities is made. When securities are bought on the exchange, the central counterparty steps in between the buyer and the seller, and becomes the seller to the buyer of the securities and the buyer to the seller of the securities. As a result both the buyer and seller have a contract with the exchange's representative, and this removes the risk that either party to the transaction will fail to carry out their side of the deal. The use of central counterparties exists on some exchanges in Europe such as futures exchanges, Tradepoint, but is not yet as well developed as in the US.

The DTCC also acts as a netting agent. Many organizations using its services continually buy and sell securities and other financial instruments. Instead of settling each transaction in securities individually, organizations might prefer to make a single net payment, or to receive a single net payment, for all the transactions they wish to settle on any particular day. By acting as a central counterparty to transactions, the DTCC also is able to provide such a netting service.

The Debt Markets and the Swaps Markets

New issues of debt commonly are arranged in conjunction with currency swaps or interest-rate swaps. The debt markets and swaps markets are interrelated, and so activity in one market can drive activity in the other.

Currency Swaps

A currency swap allows an issuer to raise money in one currency and swap its debt-repayment obligations into a second currency. For example, a company might wish to borrow dollars but its securities house/investment bank might suggest that there is a favorable opportunity to borrow Canadian dollars. The company could issue Canadian-dollar bonds and arrange a swap with a bank whereby it receives Canadian dollars from the bank to cover the loan repayments, and in exchange pays the bank in dollars. The net result is to borrow Canadian dollars but repay in dollars. This is illustrated in the following example.

Example

Alpha plc, a UK company, wishes to borrow £100 million in sterling for five years. It is advised that it would be cheaper to borrow in dollars and arrange a swap into sterling. The exchange rate is £1 = $1.50, and this rate is locked into the swap.

Analysis

Alpha would borrow $150 million and arrange a five-year currency swap into sterling with a bank, on notional principal of $150 million and at an exchange rate of £1 = $1.50.

During the term of the swap, interest payments would be exchanged at regular six-monthly intervals, Alpha paying the bank interest in sterling on a notional principal of £100 million, and the bank paying Alpha interest in dollars on a notional principal of $150 million. The dollar interest received by Alpha in the swap should be sufficient to pay its dollar-denominated bond investors.

After five years, at the end of the swap term, the bank and Alpha will reexchange principal of $150 million for £100 million. Alpha will use the $150 million received in this exchange of principal from the swap bank to redeem its maturing dollar bonds.

Interest Payments in the Currency Swap

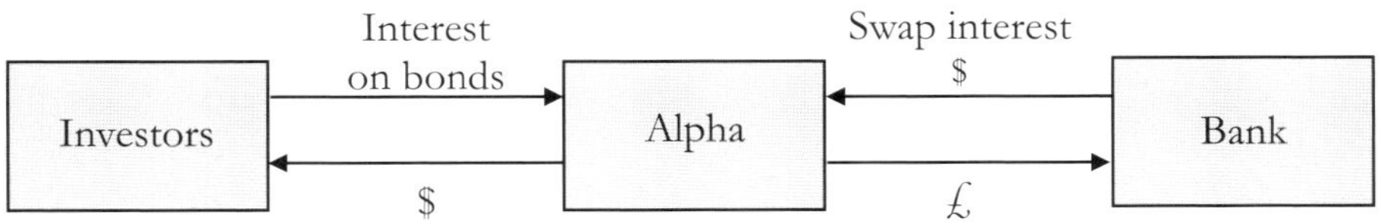

Alpha's income in dollars from the currency swap can be arranged to match its dollar-payment obligations to the bondholders, leaving Alpha as a net payer in sterling. These are the sterling payments that Alpha makes in the swap arrangement.

As a result, Alpha has borrowed in dollars but is paying interest in sterling.

Exchange of Principal at Maturity

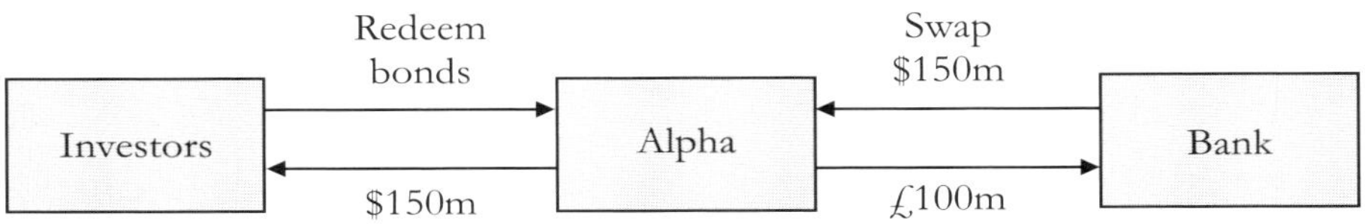

When the swap reaches the end of its term, Alpha will receive $150 million in the swap that it will use to redeem the dollar bonds. Alpha has to make a payment of £100 million in the swap, so that it has a net debt payment of £100 million.

The economic effect of the swap has been for Alpha to issue dollar bonds, but in effect to incur net payments of interest in sterling and a commitment to make a capital redemption payment at maturity, also in sterling.

Interest-Rate Swaps
The debt markets also can be driven by interest-rate swaps.

The maturity of fixed-rate issues of bonds or notes can exceed 20 years. However, a large proportion have a maturity of just five years and are swap-driven. A swap-driven issue is one in which a bank raises fixed-rate funds for the interest-rate swaps market. The advantage to the bank is that a fixed-rate debt issue combined with a swap can give it cheap variable-rate funding, at a net cost below LIBOR.

Example
Alpha Bank raises £200 million in the debt markets by issuing five-year fixed-rate bonds at 7% per annum. The bank also arranges a five-year interest-rate coupon swap with Sierra plc, a corporate customer. In the swap agreement, Sierra arranges to pay a fixed rate of 7.5% per annum on a notional principal sum of £200 million, and to receive payments in exchange from Alpha Bank at six-month LIBOR in return.

Analysis
Alpha's Bank has raised capital at a fixed rate of interest, but has converted its obligations into variable-rate payments by means of the swap. In addition, its net cost of borrowing is cheap, 0.5% below LIBOR – any borrowing cost below LIBOR can be regarded as cheap. This is illustrated in the diagram below.

Interest-Rate Swap Payments

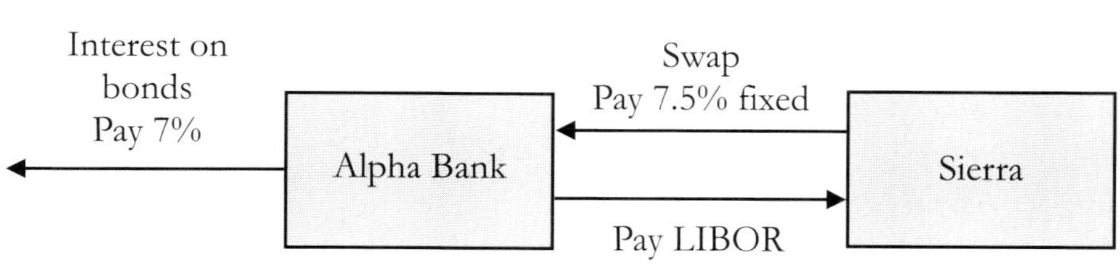

Alpha Bank's interest payments on bonds	- 7.0%
Swap	
Alpha Bank receives	+ 7.5%
Alpha Bank pays	-LIBOR
Net cost to Alpha Bank	LIBOR minus 0.50%

Sierra plc can use the same swap to obtain fixed-rate funding with a five-year maturity at a low cost by:

- borrowing at a variable rate, and
- swapping into a fixed rate.

For example, if Sierra can borrow £200 million for five years at six-month LIBOR +1% by issuing FRNs, it can use the swap to secure fixed-rate funding on £200 million for five years at 8.5%. Activity in the FRNs market therefore would be linked to the swap between Alpha Bank and Sierra.

Sierra's interest payments on bonds	- (LIBOR + 1%)
Swap	
Sierra receives	+ LIBOR
Sierra pays	- 7.5%
Net cost to Sierra	8.5%

Sierra could be forced to issue FRNs and arrange a swap to obtain fixed-rate funds. This is because issuing fixed-rate bonds could be either:

- difficult for a company of Sierra's size or credit rating, or
- achievable only at an interest rate above 8.5%.

Summary

The debt markets can be categorized in various ways:

- by types of borrower – corporates, governments
- by maturity – bonds, MTNs, CP

- by the form and method of distribution for the primary issue – public offerings and private placements
- between primary and secondary markets, and according to the nature of secondary-market trading – OTC markets
- according to whether or not issue activity is swaps-driven.

Bond Prices and Yields

A bond price is either the amount at which investors are invited to subscribe to an issue for a primary issue, or the amount that investors are willing to buy or sell the bond for in subsequent secondary-market trading.

Influences on Price

Market prices fluctuate continually. There are various factors that determine what buyers will pay or what sellers will accept for securities. The key factors are:

- the expected return (the yield to investors)
- the perceived risk, and
- the liquidity of the secondary market. Investors usually will pay more for bonds that have a liquid market than for bonds that could be difficult to resell at a fair price.

Expected Return

The expected return for interest-bearing debt securities consists of regular interest payments and the payment of the principal at maturity.

Ignoring risk and liquidity as factors that help to determine price, investors will pay more for bigger financial returns, i.e. for more interest. For example, investors will pay more for bonds with a coupon rate of 7% than for bonds with a 4% coupon because the return is higher.

It is important to understand this relationship between bond prices and yields to investors.

Example

Suppose that Alpha, an investor, buys a fixed rate bond of Tango Corporation, either in the primary issue or in the secondary market. The price at which the bond is purchased, together with the fixed rate of interest, determines the yield that Alpha can expect to receive. Alpha would not purchase the bond in the first place unless the expected yield from the bond is sufficiently high, given market conditions at the time of purchase.

Market interest rates change continually, and investors will expect a higher or lower yield on an investment, according to whether interest rates go up or down. Suppose, therefore, that some time soon after Alpha has purchased the bond, Beta, another investor, decides to buy a Tango Corporation bond in the secondary market. The price that Beta will pay could be higher or lower than the price paid by Alpha, depending on whether market interest rates have gone down or up in the meantime. Beta's investment yield on the Tango Corporation bond will differ from Alpha's yield because they purchased similar bonds at different prices.

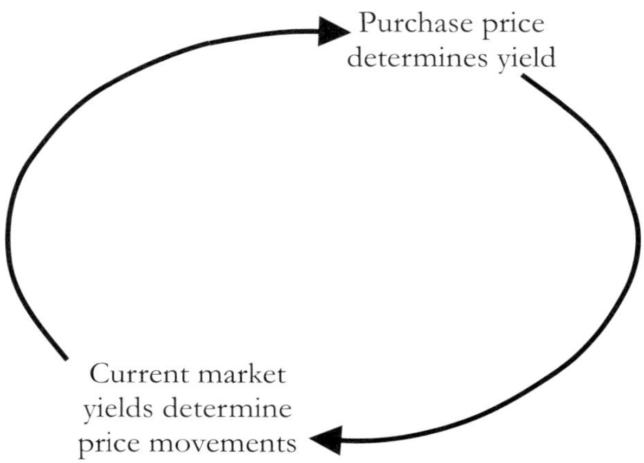

Perceived Risk

Relatively few investments are risk-free. Issuers of debt securities could default on interest payments or the payment of the debt principal at maturity. The size of return required by investors will vary according to the perceived risk. A lower yield will be obtained, for example, for a risk-free investment.

It is commonly assumed that a risk-free investment is an investment in securities of the domestic central government, provided that the government is creditworthy. Notable examples are US Treasury bonds for US investors, German government Bunds and French government bonds for investors in the euro currency zone countries, and UK government stocks for UK investors. Investors in corporate bonds will expect a higher return than from government bonds, or will pay less for a similar rate of interest.

Credit risk is measured for many bond issues by a credit rating.

Step-Up Clause

Occasionally, a bond issue has a step-up clause in its terms and conditions. This is a provision that in the event of the credit rating for the bond being downgraded for any reason, after the bond has been issued, the bond issuer will be obliged to pay a higher rate of interest on the bonds. There have been examples of a step-up clause providing for an increase of as much as 150 basis points in the coupon, in the event of a credit rating downgrade for the bonds.

Quoted Prices

The price of bonds and notes normally is quoted as a percentage of their face value. A price of 97.50, for example, means $97.50 per $100 face value for dollar bonds, or £97.50 per £100 face value for sterling bonds. The issue price for a bond might be quoted up to four decimal places. For example, an issue of bonds might be priced at 99.8667, or 102.5386.

Dealers in bonds quote two-way prices. The bid price is the price at which they will buy the bonds, and the offer or asked price is the price at which they will sell. The difference between the bid and offer prices is the dealer's spread. Financial journals usually report either the bid price or the mid-price for the bond, i.e. the average of the bid and offer prices.

Accrued Interest

For interest-bearing bonds, accrued interest is interest that has been earned on the bonds but not yet paid out to the bondholder. When interest is paid six-monthly, interest accrues for up to six months from the date of one payment to the date of the next.

Each issue of bonds has its own payment dates for interest.

Example

Interest on 6% bonds of Alpha Corporation is payable on May 1 and November 1. Interest on similar 6% bonds of Beta Corporation, a company with the same credit rating, is payable on February 20 and August 20.

Analysis

The current value of Alpha's and Beta's bonds should be the same, except that the accrued interest on each set of bonds will be different. On July 1, for example, there will be two months' accrued interest on the Alpha bonds (from May 1 to July 1) and over four months' accrued interest on the Beta bonds (from February 20 to July 1).

Clean Price and Dirty Price

Investors have to compare bond prices and yields on a like-for-like basis. However, comparing bond prices can become complex when accrued interest is taken into consideration. To get round this problem, prices exclude any value for accrued interest. The quoted prices of bonds are a clean price. However, when a transaction is settled, and a buyer pays for the bonds, the accrued interest built up but not yet payable, is added to the settlement price. The clean price plus this added interest is called the dirty price.

Example

Interest on 6% bonds issued by Gamma Corporation is payable on April

1 and October 1. An investor buys $100,000 of bonds at 97.6250 on July 1.

Interest is calculated on an actual/360-day basis.

Analysis
On July 1, 91 days of interest, payable on October 1, has built up. This accrued interest is for the period April 1 to June 30. The price paid by the investor for the bonds will be:

	$
Clean price (97.6250)	97,625.00
Accrued interest ($100,000 x 6% x 91/360)	1,516.67
Total payable (dirty price)	99,141.67

The amount of accrued interest to be added to the clean price is agreed between the back-office staff responsible for settlement, not by the bond dealers who agreed the transaction.

Cum Interest and Ex Interest
Registered bonds might be traded soon before an interest payment date. This leaves no time to register the details of the new bondholder before the interest payment is due to be made. For this reason, the interest payment may be made to the seller of the bonds, i.e. the previous bondholder.

When bonds are purchased and an interest payment is due soon after, it is important to establish whether the purchaser will be entitled to the next payment of interest, or whether the payment should be made to the previous owner. For example, suppose that some bonds that pay interest on March 10 and September 10 are sold by Alpha to Beta on March 8, two days before the next interest payment is due. It is important to establish whether Alpha or Beta is entitled to the payment. In practise, there are bond market rules for deciding whether bonds are sold:

- cum interest (cum int), i.e. the buyer is entitled to the next payment of interest, or
- ex interest (ex int), i.e. the seller retains the right to receive the next interest payment.

If bonds are sold cum interest, the buyer must pay the seller for the accrued interest. If they are sold ex interest, there is no accrued interest to pay and the settlement price is the clean price.

Bonds will be sold cum interest until a specified time before the next interest-payment date when they go ex interest for a short time.

Broken Periods

When bonds are sold, the accrued interest is unlikely to be for a round number of months. The interest accrued might be calculated as the number of months at 30 days per month plus the number of calendar days in the broken month up to the date of the transaction.

Example

A 5% bond pays interest on March 16 and September 16. Bonds to the face value of 1,000 euros are sold on July 7. Interest is calculated on a 30/360-day convention.

Analysis

Accrued interest is for 14 days in March (30 – 16 = 14, because every month has 30 days), three months April, May and June, and seven days in July.

Number of days = 14 + (3 x 30) + 7 = 111 days
Accrued interest = €1,000 x 10% x (111/360) = €30.83.

How Is a Clean Price Established?

The clean market price of a bond is the value of the future income stream from the bond (interest and redemption value), discounted to a present value at the rate of return that investors are willing to accept. This present value is the clean price.

For example, suppose a company issues five-year bonds, redeemable at par, with a coupon rate of 8% per annum and interest payable every six months. The issue price of the bonds, per $100 nominal value, will be at the market's valuation of an income stream of $4 every six months for five years plus $100 at the end of five years. This future income should be discounted at the rate of return that investors will require from the bond to determine the issue price/clean price.

Discounting arithmetic is beyond the scope of this book. Briefly, each future item of income – interest payments and the redemption payment at maturity – is multiplied by a discount factor to convert it to a present value. The discount factor is $1/(1 + r)^n$, where n is the number of time periods in the future that the income will be received and r is the return, per time period, that investors require from the bond. This is expressed as a proportion, e.g. 5% = 0.05.

When interest is paid annually, r is an annual rate of return and n represents the number of years in the future that the income will be received. When interest is paid six-monthly, r is a half-year rate of return and n represents six-month periods.

Example
Loan stock with an 8% coupon has four years remaining to maturity, when it will be redeemed at par. Interest is paid every six months. Bond dealers are pricing the loan stock on the assumption that the yield to bondholders should be 6% per annum (3% per half-year).

Analysis
Bond dealers will price the loan stock by discounting the bond's future income stream to a present value. The discount rate is the required six-monthly yield of 3%, and the discount factor is $1/(1.03)^n$.

After	Time period (n =)	Income	Amount	Discount factor at 3%	Present value
6 months	1	Interest	4	$1/(1.03)^1$	3.88
1 year	2	Interest	4	$1/(1.03)^2$	3.77
18 months	3	Interest	4	$1/(1.03)^3$	3.66
2 years	4	Interest	4	$1/(1.03)^4$	3.55
30 months	5	Interest	4	$1/(1.03)^5$	3.45
3 years	6	Interest	4	$1/(1.03)^6$	3.35
42 months	7	Interest	4	$1/(1.03)^7$	3.25
4 years	8	Interest	4	$1/(1.03)^8$	3.16
4 years	8	Principal	100	$1/(1.03)^8$	78.94
				Total	107.01

Dealers will price the bonds at 107.01. This is the clean price of the bond.

Measuring the Yield on Interest-Bearing Securities

The yield on interest-bearing securities before tax, i.e. the gross yield, consists of two elements:

- interest and
- redemption of the loan principal at maturity.

The yield usually is expressed as a percentage annual rate on the cost of the investment. The return or yield for each individual investor varies according to:

- when the bonds were purchased, and the period to maturity
- the price paid for the bonds
- the interest rate
- the redemption value of the bonds, and
- the investor's taxation position.

To compare the yields obtainable on different bonds in the market, it is useful to look at their pre-tax or gross yields. These are the yields before tax that investors would receive if they were to purchase the bonds at their current market price.

A yield can be defined and expressed in three different ways:

- as a coupon yield
- as a current yield, and
- as a redemption yield.

The coupon yield and current yield consider only the annual interest on the debt. The redemption yield takes into account both the interest and the eventual payment of the loan principal at maturity.

Coupon Yield and Current Yield

The *coupon yield* is the coupon rate of interest. On 5% loan stock, for example, the coupon yield or coupon is 5%.

The *current yield* is the coupon rate of interest, as a percentage of the current market value of the security.

$$\text{Current Yield} = \frac{\text{Coupon Rate}}{\text{Market Price}} \times 100\%$$

Example

6% bonds have a current market price of 101.50. The current yield is therefore:

$$\frac{6}{101.50} \times 100\% = 5.91\%$$

Redemption Yield

A bond's redemption yield is the yield for the bondholder, based on the bond's current market value, that takes account of both future interest payments and the loan principal repayment at maturity. It is the average annual rate of return that the bondholder will receive over the remaining period to maturity, expressed as a percentage of the bond's current market value.

Example
A 7% sterling bond that pays interest semi-annually, has three years remaining to maturity when it will be redeemed at par. Its current market price is 97.39.

Analysis
The redemption yield on the loan stock is the average annual yield at which an investor will receive the following cash flows to maturity, on an investment of $97.39.

After		**Cash flow** **$**
6 months		3.5
1 year		3.5
18 months		3.5
2 years		3.5
30 months		3.5
3 years	- interest	3.5
	- loan principal	100.0

Redemption yields can be calculated by discount arithmetic, although specialist calculators can be used. The method of calculation is similar in concept to the technique for calculating a clean price for a bond that was illustrated previously.

The redemption yield is the rate of interest at which the future income from the bond should be discounted, so that the present value of this future income is equal to the current value of the bond.

In this example the redemption yield is 4% per half year, as shown in the table below.

After	Time period (n =)	Income	Amount	Discount factor at 4% per half year	Present value $
6 months	1	Interest	3.50	1/(1.04)	3.37
1 year	2	Interest	3.50	1/(1.04)	3.24
18 months	3	Interest	3.50	1/(1.04)	3.11
2 years	4	Interest	3.50	1/(1.04)	2.99
30 months	5	Interest	3.50	1/(1.04)	2.88
3 years	6	Interest	3.50	1/(1.04)	2.77
3 years	6	Principal	100.00	1/(1.04)	79.03
				Total	97.39

In the bond markets, the redemption yield on this bond would be quoted as 8% per annum, twice the six-monthly yield of 4%, rather than at the more accurate compounded annual yield of 8.16%.

Yields on bonds change regularly in daily trading as the price of the bond goes up or down.

Current Yield and Redemption Yield

The best measure of a bond yield is the redemption yield. This takes into consideration all the expected returns to the bondholder, such as loan principal and interest and not just interest.

Current yield has some uses, however.

- It is a measure of the short-term returns on the bond, i.e. the interest payments. This can be important for an investor's cash flows.
- It is easier to calculate than redemption yield.

For bonds with a short maturity, the redemption yield is strongly influenced by the capital gain or loss on redemption. For bonds with a long maturity, however, current yield and redemption yield will be roughly the same because the capital gain or loss on redemption, many years in the future, will be a relatively insignificant influence on the redemption yield.

Example
Two issues of 8% loan stock have a market value of 95, and each pays interest annually. Issue C matures in two years, and Issue D matures in 15 years. Both are redeemable at par.

Analysis
The current yield on both securities is 8.42% (8/95 x 100%).

The workings are not shown here, but the redemption yield on the short-term bond, Issue C, is about 11% per annum. The redemption yield on the longer-term bond, Issue D is much lower at about 8% per annum.

The higher redemption yield on Issue C compared to Issue D is because of its shorter term to maturity. The capital gain on redemption is 5 (100-95) for both bonds, but this is more significant if it happens in just two years' time rather than after 15 years. The redemption yield on Issue D that has a long term to maturity, is very close to its current yield.

When a security's market price is at a discount to its nominal value, its redemption yield will be higher than the current yield. When its market price is at a premium to the redemption value, usually par, the redemption yield will be lower than the current yield.

Changes in Interest Rates and Bond Prices

When interest rates go up or down, the secondary market price of fixed-rate bonds also will change. Suppose, for example, that investors require a yield of 6% on a 15-year issue of bonds. The coupon rate on the bonds is also 6%, therefore the market price of the bonds is 100, i.e. par.

If market interest rates go up from 6% to 9% existing bondholders will continue to receive $6 fixed-rate interest per annum on each $100 nominal value of bonds. However, new buyers of the bonds in the secondary market, who will require a yield of 9%, will pay only the price that gives them this yield. The market price of the bonds will fall to a level at which the gross yield is 9%. Investors who bought the bonds at

100 when market interest rates were 6%, will suffer a loss in capital value on their investment.

The new price of the bonds can be estimated from the formula:

$$\text{Market value} = \frac{\text{Interest per annum on bonds}}{\text{Market rate of interest}}$$

In this example, the new market price of the bonds following a change in interest rates from 6% to 9% (0.09) will be approximately:

$$\frac{16}{0.09} = 66.67$$

While this price formula gives only an approximation of the market price, it illustrates the key principle that when market interest rates go down, secondary market prices of existing bonds go up. Conversely, when interest rates go up, bond prices fall.

Interest-Rate Changes and Bond Prices

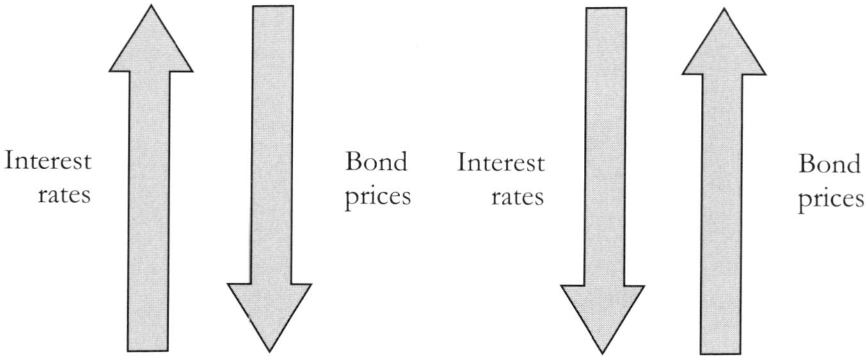

How Are Corporate Bond Yields Determined?

The yield that investors require from corporate bonds is higher than the yield obtainable on government securities with the same maturity. Corporate bond yields can be set at a margin or spread above government bond yields. Because there can be many different government bonds in issue with similar maturities, particular reference stocks are used to establish the current yield on government bonds for a given maturity.

The required yield varies according to the maturity of the bonds. The rates that apply at each maturity combine to produce a yield curve. A yield curve can be tabulated or shown in a graph form.

Maturity	**Yield on government securities %**
2 years	6.75
3 years	6.90
5 years	7.25
7 years	7.60
10 years	7.90
15 years	8.00
20 years	8.00

Yield Curve

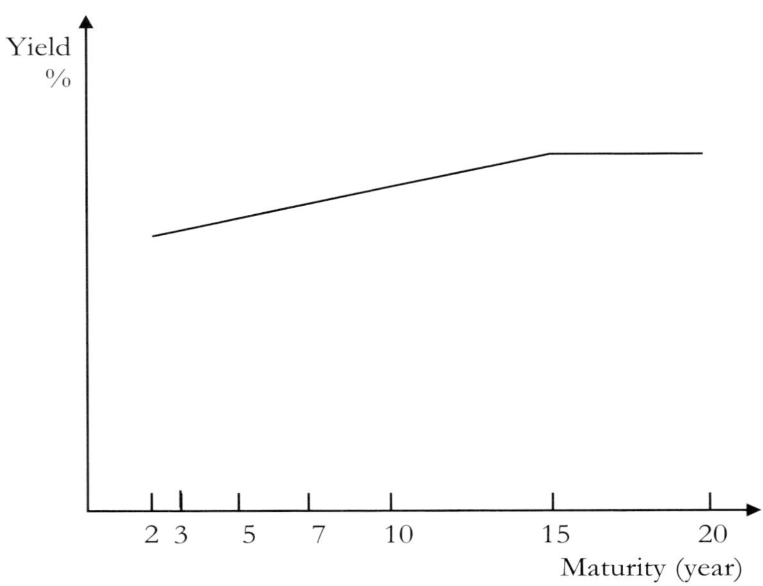

The slope of the yield curve is upwards, flattening out between 15 and 20 years maturities, because the yield is higher for longer maturities.

An upward-sloping curve is said to be normal because investors usually expect a higher yield for a long-term investment of funds. However, if long-term yields are much higher than short-term yields the yield curve is said to be supernormal.

When short-term yields are higher than long-term yields, the yield curve is downward-sloping or inverse.

For each issue of corporate bonds the market will take a view of what its yield to investors should be as a margin above the yield curve for government bonds. The size of this margin will vary according to:

- the maturity of the stock. The margin will be wider for longer maturities
- the credit risk. The spread above the yield on government bonds will be narrowest for issues with a triple-A credit rating.

Current Maturity and Price Volatility

When market rates of interest change, bond prices also will change. Price volatility refers to the extent of the price change. Volatility will vary between different bond issues. Some bond issues are more volatile in price than others. One reason for greater price volatility is long-term maturity. The price change in response to a change in market interest rates is greater for securities with a long term to maturity. For short-coupon bonds, the price effect of an interest-rate change is smaller. This is because the yield on short-coupon bonds is more strongly influenced by the capital gain or loss on redemption that is unaffected by rises or falls in market rates of interest.

Example
An investor holds two bonds. The current redemption yield is 8% on each.

Bond E is 6% loan stock with one year to maturity. It is redeemable at par, and its current market price is 98.15.

Bond F is 6% loan stock with a further ten years to maturity. It is redeemable at par, and its current market price is 86.58.

Market rates of interest go up, and the redemption yield that investors now require goes up to 9% for both bonds.

Analysis
Because interest rates have gone up, bond prices will fall. The percentage fall in price will be greater for Bond F than for Bond E because Bond F has a longer term remaining before maturity.

Although calculations are not shown, the new market prices of the securities should be approximately as follows.

	Old price	**Approximate new price**	**Approximate fall in price**	**Approximate % fall in price**
Bond E	98.15	97.25	0.90	0.9
Bond F	86.58	80.75	5.83	6.7

When interest rates fall, the opposite effect occurs. Bonds with a long term to maturity should rise in price by more in percentage terms, than bonds with short maturities.

Coupon Rate and Price Volatility

The volatility of a bond's market price also depends on its coupon rate. A bond with a low coupon has greater price volatility than a similar bond with a high coupon.

Example
An investor holds two bonds, Bond G and Bond H. Both have five years remaining to maturity and are redeemable at par. Bond G is 5% loan stock and has a current market price of 87.84. Bond H is 10% loan stock

and has a current market price of 108.12.

The current market yield on five-year loan stock is 8%.

Analysis
Suppose the yield falls from 8% to 6%. The market price of the bonds will rise. Although the calculations are not shown, the change in prices should be approximately as follows:

	Old price	**Approximate new price**	**Approximate fall in price**	**Approximate % fall in price**
Bond G	87.84	95.74	7.90	9.0
Bond H	108.12	117.06	8.94	8.3

The percentage change in price is greater for Bond G that has the lower coupon rate of interest.

Floating-Rate Notes

The market price of variable-rate bonds (FRNs) normally should remain close to par. This is because the interest paid to investors will rise or fall in step with movements in market rates of interest. However, if there is a change in the credit or investment risk with the bonds, and investors require a higher or lower yield to compensate them for the change in risk, the market price will change.

Discount Securities

Some short-term debt securities, including commercial paper, are issued on a discount basis, i.e. they are issued at a discount to their face value and redeemed at par. No interest is paid, and the yield to investors comes from the capital gain on redemption. For example 60-day commercial paper could be issued at a price of 98.36 and redeemed at par. The capital gain on redemption for the investor would be 1.64 per 100 nominal value. This gain is in effect an interest yield of 10% on a 60-day investment of 98.36 (60/360 x 10% x 98.36 = 1.64).

Commercial-paper pricing is described in Chapter 7.

Pricing a Bond Issue

When a new issue of bonds is made, an important decision is the selection of the issue price and coupon rate of interest.

- If the interest rate is high in relation to the issue price, investors will be keen to buy at that price subject to a satisfactory credit rating and expectations that the secondary market will be liquid. After the issue, the price of the bonds should rise in the secondary market.
- If the coupon rate is too low for the issue price, investors will be reluctant to buy at that price and the issue will be under-subscribed. If the issue is underwritten, many of the bonds will be left in the hands of the underwriters and sub-underwriters. In the subsequent secondary market, the bond price will fall below the issue price, so the pricing decision is left as late as possible before the bond issue is launched and the selling process begins.

Bond Yields and Money Market Yields

It was explained in Chapter 1 how interest on bonds is calculated differently, according to the interest-rate convention used.

The same complexity applies to the calculation of interest on money market or short-term financial instruments. A yield of 6% on a bond and a yield of 6% on a money market instrument can mean different amounts of interest.

Interest rates quoted on a bond basis may assume a 360-day year or 30-day month. In comparison, rates quoted on a money market basis may assume a 365-day year with interest calculated on the actual number of days in the period from issue to maturity.

To compare yields between bonds and money market instruments, it may be necessary to convert a yield on a bond from a bond basis to a money market basis. To do this, it would be necessary to multiply by a factor of 360/365.

Similarly, it may be necessary to convert the money market yield on a financial instrument to a bond market yield, to compare the yield of the money market instrument with the yield on the bond. To convert from a money market basis to a bond basis, the factor is 365/360.

- Money market basis = Bond basis x 360/365
- Bond basis = Money market basis x 365/360

Example

An issue of ten-year bonds offers a yield of 10% per annum. An issue of commercial paper, issued on May 1 and maturing on August 1, also offers a yield of 10%. The CP has a maturity of 92 days. Bond interest is calculated on a 30/360-day basis.

Analysis

Because both securities yield 10%, it could be supposed that they will earn the same amount of interest in the period May 1 to August 1. This is not the case, however. The CP is a money market instrument that earns interest for 92 days. The bond earns interest for just 90 days (3 months).

During the term of the CP the interest for the investor will be 25.21 per 100 invested (92/365 x 10% of 100). In the same three-month or 92-day period, interest on the bonds per 100 invested would be just 25 (90/360 x 10% of 100).

A money market rate of 10% is the equivalent of a bond rate of 10.14% (10% x 365/360). Similarly, a bond rate of 10% is the equivalent of a money market rate of 9.86% (10% x 360/365).

Taxation of Income from Bonds

The description of yield so far has ignored taxation on bondholders' income from interest that can influence decisions about investing in bonds.

The redemption yield for an individual investor, after deducting taxation on the income, is the investor's net redemption yield. This varies according to the investor's tax position.

Withholding Tax and the Yield to Investors

Investors generally prefer to receive interest gross, without deduction of tax, and to settle their tax liabilities on investment income at a later time.

Withholding tax is tax on interest or dividends that must be deducted at source by the issuer of the securities and paid to the government.

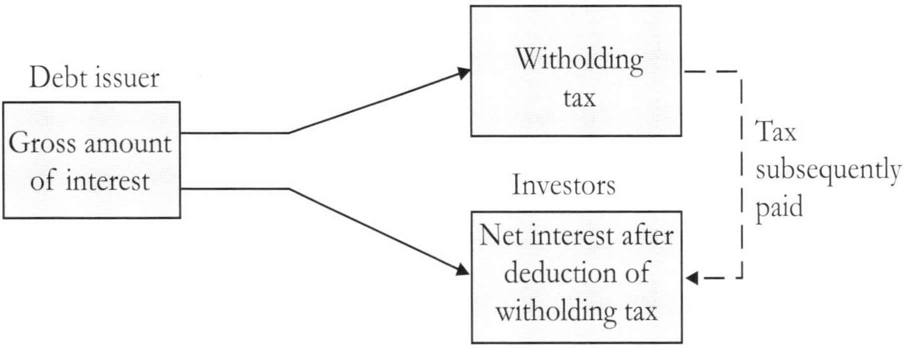

Withholding tax can be a particular concern for foreign investors in domestic bonds of another country's bond market. Interest on bonds by a company in one country could be subject to deduction of withholding tax when paid to foreign bondholders. The tax often is paid back to the bondholders by the government, but not until some time later. In the meantime, the government has the benefit of interest-free cash, and the investors are deprived of the reinvestment potential of their money.

Example
Beta, a UK company, is issuing 10% loan notes with a maturity of three years. The issue price is at par. Interest is payable every six months.

Suppose an overseas investor is considering whether to buy the stock, but is concerned about a 20% withholding tax. The tax would be recoverable, but not for 12 months after the interest-payment date.

Analysis
Every six months, Beta will pay gross interest of £5 per £100 nominal value of loan notes. If withholding tax is 20%, one-fifth of the interest payable, £1 per £100 of notes, would go to the government, and the investor would receive just £4 per £100. Although the tax will be repaid after 12 months, the investor has lost the use of the £1 during this period when it could have been reinvested to earn more money.

One of the attractions of eurobonds for international investors is that no withholding tax is deducted at source by the bond issuer and interest is paid gross. To avoid the possibility of having to deduct withholding tax at source on interest payments to foreign bondholders, companies might prefer to issue bonds in the eurobond market rather tan in their own domestic bond market.

Summary

The issue price of bonds, and their subsequent secondary-market price, is determined by the yield required by investors. The required yield is influenced by

- the credit risk from investing in the bonds
- the maturity of the bonds
- the expected liquidity of the secondary market in the bonds.

Bond prices are the present value of future income from the bonds, discounted at the rate of return (redemption yield) required by investors. Yields on corporate bonds are at a margin above yields on government bonds with a similar maturity. The government bond market, in this respect, is a major influence on the corporate bond market.

When interest rates rise or are expected to rise, bond prices will fall. When interest rates fall or are expected to fall, bond prices will rise. Some bond issues have greater price volatility than others. Major influences on price volatility are the term to maturity of the bond and its coupon rate.

Although yields in the bond markets are gross yields, decisions by investors to purchases bond issues will be influenced by taxation. Bonds that pay interest gross, without deduction of withholding tax, will be more attractive than bonds for which tax is deductible at source on interest payments.

Information about bond prices and yields is provided on information screens and in the financial press. Information that might be given particular prominence is summarized below.

Bond issuer **Item**	**ABCD Corp**	**XYZ Corp**	**Mango Corp**
Redemption date	05/08	10/08	04/09
Coupon	8.00%	7.38%	5.86%
S & P rating	A -	BBB -	AAA
Moody's rating	Baa1	Baa3	Aaa
Bid price	105.6291	99.2422	99.2510
Bid yield	6.99%	7.50%	5.97%
Spread over govt. bonds	+ 1.76%	+ 2.27%	+ 0.74%

Making a Corporate Bond Issue

Introduction

The procedures for making a bond issue vary between capital markets, according to the regulations of each market. In highly regulated domestic markets such as the US and the UK, the intention to make a new issue must be notified to the authorities. In the US new issues of bonds and notes must be registered with the Securities and Exchange Commission (SEC).

Important concerns for an issuer of bonds may be:

- the speed and flexibility with which an issue can be made, and
- the costs of making an issue.

Making an issue can be lengthy, taking as long as several months, and also can be expensive. A major cause of delay and expense is the preparation and approval of documentation for the issue.

When deciding whether to invest in a new issue investors must have information about the issuer and its reasons for wanting capital so for every new issue, there must be a document that provides this information. The contents of any such offer document or prospectus, that are specified by the rules of the market regulator, for example the stock exchange, vary between different markets and types of issue.

This chapter describes aspects of making a bond issue in the eurobond market. They have many similarities with issuing bonds in other corporate bond markets.

Eurobonds are bonds that are distributed internationally when issued and subsequently traded by dealers in several international financial centers. The international bond markets are now an important source of funds for many large banks and non-bank corporates, as well as national governments and government agencies. Eurobond issues are made mostly through telephone sales and by the placement of bonds with client investors by a group of selling banks.

The Parties Involved in a Eurobond Issue

The parties to a eurobond issue are:

- the issuer
- a lead manager
- a syndicate of co-managers
- a fiscal agent or a trustee
- a principal paying agent and other paying agents
- a listing agent, if the bonds are to be listed
- a depository
- legal advisers
- auditors
- investors.

The **currency** of the issue must be a freely traded international currency such as the dollar, euro, yen, sterling, Swiss franc, Australian dollar or Canadian dollar. The issuer does not have to issue bonds in the currency that it wants to obtain finance: an issuer is able to raise funds in one currency and switch into a different currency using a currency swap.

Although the eurobond market is an international bond market, it is a misconception to suppose that a bond issuer must issue bonds in a foreign currency. A UK bond issuer, for example, may well issue bonds denominated in dollars or euros, but equally it could issue sterling-denominated bonds. The distinguishing feature of a eurobond or international bond issue is that it should be sold to investors in many countries by a syndicate of banks in different countries.

Lead Manager

Every bond issue has a lead manager. The lead manager is responsible for:

- arranging the issue
- advising the bond issuer
- managing the issue process from the time of its appointment as lead manager until the bonds have been issued and the funds raised.

A company wishing to make a bond issue can invite a number of investment banks to bid for the role of lead manager. The choice of lead manager will be based on the bids received and on the reputation or standing in the market of each bidder. Each bidder will be asked to indicate the price at which they believe they can issue the bonds, and the size of their fees.

The lead manager will advise the issuer on matters such as:

- the structure and size of the issue
- the currency of issue
- the interest rate and issue price
- obtaining credit ratings for the bonds
- terms and conditions that might have to be included in the bond issue to make the bonds acceptable to investors.

When the bonds are to be listed and accepted for trading on a stock exchange, it is usual for the lead manager to act as the listing agent.

Syndicate of Co-Managers

When appointed, the lead manager for a eurobond issue must assemble an international syndicate of other investment banks to co-manage the issue. The syndicate will make the bonds available to investors in different countries using their lists of client contacts.

The co-managers fulfill two functions:

- to sell the bonds either directly to investors or by placing bonds with other banks that will sell to their clients, and perhaps
- to underwrite the issue, or to find other banks that would be willing to underwrite the issue.

Arranging a Eurobond Issue

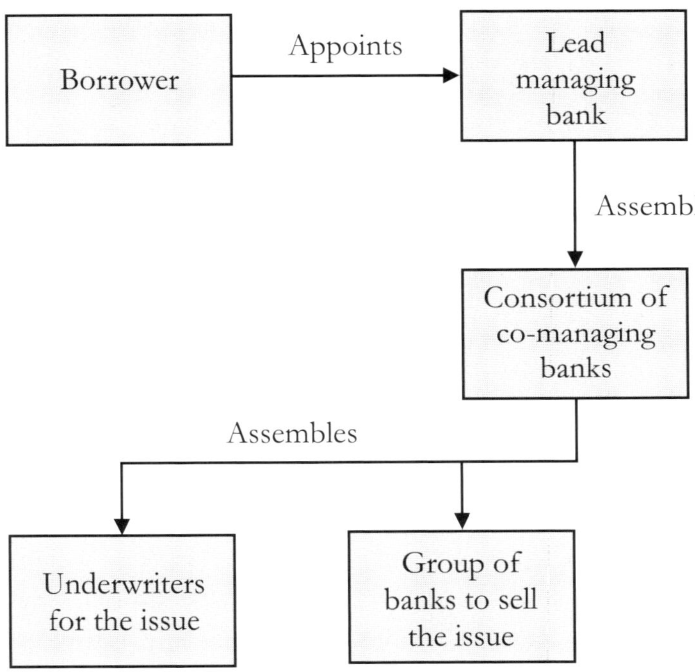

Underwriting

An underwriter of a bond issue agrees to buy up a quantity of bonds in the issue at an agreed price in the event that investors cannot be found to buy them. In return, the underwriter receives a commission that might be about 3.5 to 5 basis points, i.e. 0.035% to 0.05% of the value of the bonds they agree to underwrite.

- If the issue is successful, all the bonds will be sold to investors, and the underwriters will not be required to buy any of them.

- If the issue is not successful, some bonds will be left unsold, and these must be taken up by the underwriters, in proportion to the quantity of bonds they have underwritten.

When bonds are left in the hands of underwriters, the underwriters are likely to want to sell them off as soon as they can, even at a loss. These bonds will hang over the market until they are eventually sold, depressing the secondary-market price for the bonds.

Selling the Bonds

The process of selling eurobonds involves making a book. This means simply that the selling banks build up a list of investors who are willing to buy the bonds. The banks that organize the book are known as the bookrunners for the issue.

The traditional way of selling eurobonds is by phone to investors on the selling bank's list of clients. In 2000, there were some e-bond issues of eurobonds in which the selling banks offered bonds to investors via the internet. E-bond issues may become more common in the future.

Fees and Expenses

The lead manager and bond issuer agree on the fees that will be charged. The fees are negotiable, but are likely to vary with the name and credit standing of the bond issuer. Higher fees will be charged for bond issues with a long maturity.

- There is a management fee, typically about 37.5 to 50 basis points. For a $400-million bond issue with a management fee of 50 basis points, the cost to the issuer would be $2 million (0.50% x $400 million). The lead manager will retain a part of this fee, and pass on the rest to its co-managers.
- Underwriting commissions are an additional cost, and may be about 37.5 to 50 basis points.
- A selling commission is paid to the institutions that sell the bonds. This could be around 75 to 150 basis points of the amount of bonds allotted to each selling institution.

The bond issuer also will be required to pay for other costs, such as the legal expenses of the issue.

Fiscal Agent or Trustee

A eurobond issue has either a fiscal agent or a trustee. It does not have both.

Fiscal Agent

A fiscal agent is appointed by the issuer under a fiscal-agency agreement, and is an agent of the issuer.

The prime responsibility of the fiscal agent usually is to act as the principal paying agent and pay interest and principal at redemption, to the bondholders. However, there are also certain other administrative responsibilities, such as arranging the publication of notices to bondholders.

Trustee

A eurobond issue that does not have a fiscal agent will have a trustee. A trustee is appointed by the bond issuer, and the trustee's fees and expenses are paid by the issuer. However, the trustee's duties are to the bondholders, not the issuer.

The powers and duties of the trustee are set out in the **trust deed**. In broad terms, the duties are to look after the interests of the bondholders. The powers and duties of the trustee may include:

- the duty to act on behalf of the bondholders in the event of default
- the power to wave minor events of default
- the power to negotiate an arrangement with the issuer in the event of default.

In addition, under common law, a trustee owes a duty of care to the bondholders, and to act with due diligence on their behalf.

Some organizations such as trust corporations, specialize in acting as trustees for bond issues.

Trust arrangements usually are not recognized in countries, including many in Europe, that have a civil-law jurisdiction because trusts are a common-law concept. Even when the governing law for the issue is English, and the bond issuer has a choice between a fiscal agent and a trustee, the preference usually is for a fiscal agent. This is because a fiscal agent is cheaper.

Principal Paying Agent and Other Paying Agents

A paying agent is a bank acting as an agent for the bond issuer to pay out the interest on the bonds to the bondholders, and to pay the principal when the bonds are redeemed. The issuer must make the money available to the paying agent in time to make the payments.

Because eurobonds are held by investors indifferent countries, it is usual to have:

- a principal paying agent in one country, and
- a paying agent in each of several other countries.

For example, a UK-based multinational company issuing bonds through a Dutch finance subsidiary might appoint a principal paying agent in London and other paying agents in Luxembourg and Zurich.

Bondholders can choose which paying agent to use. The principal paying agent acts as a paying agent in its own country, and in addition co-ordinates the activities of the other paying agents. For example, the bond issuer will make the money for an interest payment available to the principal paying agent who will make the money available to the other paying agents.

When the bonds are bearer bonds issued in certificate form, a paying agent will make a payment of interest against presentation of the interest coupon by the bondholder or bondholder's agent. Redemption of the principal at maturity is against presentation of the certificate. When bearer bonds are held in book-entry form, in Clearstream or Euroclear, payments are made through these organizations into the accounts of their participants.

Depository

The functions of a central securities depository are described in Chapter 2.

Although Clearstream and Euroclear maintain records of the ownership of bearer bonds in book-entry form, there is also either an underlying bond document or underlying bond certificates. These are held for safekeeping by a depository bank that operates in tandem with Euroclear and Clearstream.

Terms and Conditions of a Eurobond

Whether a eurobond takes a global form or a definitive form, it includes a set of terms and conditions.

The documents in which the terms and conditions are shown include:

- the global bond, if the bond is in this form rather than in certificate form
- on the reverse side of each bond certificate, if the bonds are in certificate form
- in the listing particulars or other offer document.

The Range of Terms and Conditions

Terms and conditions that are of particular interest to eurobond investors relate mainly to:

- the interest payable on the bond
- when the bonds may be redeemed, and under what circumstances
- the credit rating for the issue, and the requirement for the bonds to have a rating from one or two credit-rating agencies
- how the rights of the bondholders will rank with the rights of other creditors and holders of other debt instruments of the issuer in an event of default.

The terms and conditions for a bond issue will vary to some extent between different issues according to conditions in the bond markets at the time of the issue. Investors might voice their concerns about bond investments to banks that specialize in bond issues, and in this way the lead manager for an issue might draw up the terms and conditions for a new issue to reflect current investor sentiment.

Checklist of Terms and Conditions of a Eurobond

The terms and conditions of a bond vary to some extent between issues, and according to the type of issue, e.g. a straight fixed-rate bond, a floating-rate note, a convertible bond, etc. The following checklist provides a brief guide to many of the terms and conditions that will be found in most issues.

Item	Comment
Description of the bond	When bonds are issued in certificate form, the main details such as the name of the bond issuer, amount of the bond issue, face value of the bond certificate, interest rate, maturity, ISIN number, etc., are shown on the front of the certificate. The terms and conditions will specify the form of the bond, such as bearer, registered, global, the denominations in which the bonds are issued such as \$10,000 and \$50,000, and how title in the bonds is transferred, in the case of bearer bonds, by delivery.

Item	**Comment** (cont)
Status clause	The status of the bonds will be specified whether the bonds are secured, unsecured or subordinated debt. It is usual for eurobonds to be unsecured and to rank equally, *pari passu*, with all other unsecured creditors of the issuer.
Negative pledge clause	See below
Interest clause	This clause specifies the interest rate payable on the bond, and the interest-rate convention that will be used. Note: Interest on eurobonds currently is paid gross, without any deduction of withholding tax by the issuer.
Payments	A clause in the terms and conditions will specify how payments to bondholders will be made through the paying agent(s). For bearer bonds in definitive form, payment will be made on the delivery to a paying agent of the appropriate interest-rate coupon or, on redemption, the bond certificate.
Redemption	A redemption clause will specify the circumstances in which the bond may be redeemed by the issuer. This will include redemption at par at maturity, but there also may be provisions for earlier redemption. The bondholders may have a put option.
Repurchase	The bondholder may have a call option, giving it the right to repurchase the bonds before their redemption date. The conditions for repurchase will be specified.
Covenants	See below.
Events of default	See below

Item	Comment (cont)
Replacement of certificates and coupons	A clause in the terms and conditions will deal with the replacement of certificates and interest coupons that have been lost, destroyed or damaged.
Bondholders meetings	The terms and conditions will specify the circumstances in which meetings of bondholders may be called.
Notices	These are the notices that the bond issuer is required to give to the bondholders, and the form that these notices should take.
Governing law and jurisdiction	This is the final clause in the terms and conditions. Most eurobonds are issued under English governing law, and are subject to jurisdiction of English courts.

Events of Default

The terms and conditions of a eurobond will specify the circumstances in which an event of default will occur. These circumstances are fewer and less restrictive than for a typical commercial loan agreement. An event of default will occur when the issuer:

- fails to make a payment of interest on time, although the issuer usually is allowed a fairly lengthy grace period, perhaps about two weeks
- fails to make a payment of principal on time
- breaches a covenant
- becomes insolvent.

There may be a *cross-default clause* whereby the bond issuer will be in default if it defaults under any loan agreement or with another bond issue. However, any such cross-default clause will be subject to a much higher minimum threshold level than in a typical commercial loan agreement. Cross-default will not occur unless the issuer defaults on other loans or bonds above a specified threshold amount (in aggregate).

When an event of default occurs, the bondholders can, if they wish, demand the immediate repayment of the bonds, together with any unpaid accrued interest. However, the bondholders might prefer to allow the bondholder an opportunity to rectify the problem.

Bondholders deal with the bond issuer through an authorized representative, the trustee or the fiscal agent.

Bond Covenants

An event of default will occur if the issuer breaches a covenant. At one time it was unusual for eurobonds to have any covenants in their terms and conditions. Even now, eurobonds have covenants that are fewer in number and also less onerous than covenants in a typical commercial loan agreement.

The inclusion of covenants in eurobond issues grew out of the recognition of event risk, and the experience of defaults and losses for bondholders in the market. Three covenants that are common in eurobonds are:

- a negative pledge
- a disposal of assets clause or event-risk clause, and
- a gearing ratio or leverage ratio.

Negative Pledge

A negative pledge for a eurobond is less onerous than a negative pledge in a typical commercial loan agreement. The issuer undertakes that, so long as the bonds remain outstanding and have not been redeemed, it will not create any new charge or other form of security over its assets or revenues to secure any new debt unless the bonds have equal security. A negative pledge in a eurobond is simply an undertaking by the issuer not to issue any new debt in the future that has better security. Because eurobonds usually are unsecured, the issuer undertakes not to raise any new secured debt so long as the bonds remain outstanding, unless the bonds also are given equal security.

Disposal-of-Assets Covenant

A disposal-of-assets covenant sets a limit on the amount of assets that the bond issuer is permitted to dispose of while the bonds remain outstanding. The limit on disposals might be 30% of the gross assets of the company and its group. For example, an international company with assets of $100 billion issue bonds with a disposal-of-assets clause in the covenants. If the covenant set a limit to disposals of 25%, the bond issuer would be in breach of its covenant if its assets were to fall below $75 billion.

A disposal-of-assets clause, when used, is intended to prevent a break up of the company without reference to the bondholders. A significant disposal of assets by the bond issuer would affect the credit rating for the bonds, and the marketability and value of the bonds.

Gearing-Ratio Covenant

The bond issuer may give an undertaking to restrict its total borrowings to no more than a specified percentage of its net worth. For example, a bond issuer might undertake to limit its total borrowings to no more than 200% of the value of its shareholder capital and reserves – its net worth.

A gearing-ratio covenant for a bond is similar to a gearing-ratio covenant for a loan agreement, but the total borrowing ceiling in a bond issue usually is set quite high. A bond issuer should not be expected to breach this covenant unless it were to get into serious financial difficulties or unless, for some reason, it increased its borrowings quite dramatically.

Issuing the Bonds

Eurobonds are issued in compliance with IPMA Recommendations. These do not have statutory backing, but organizations that act as managers in a eurobond issue usually are members of the IPMA, and follow the recommendations.

The length of time from giving a mandate to the lead manager (launching the issue) to closing normally takes five to six weeks, but may be shorter. IPMA rules include guidelines as to how long each stage in the process should take, and the lead manager is expected to monitor progress and ensure that unnecessary delays are avoided.

Stages in a Bond Issue

The main stages in the issue and listing of a eurobond issue are:

- giving a mandate to the lead bank
- due diligence
- preparing the documentation
- the roadshow: marketing the issue
- launching the issue and forming the syndicate
- obtaining a listing for the bonds
- signing the subscription agreement
- closing.

Some of these stages overlap each other, and run concurrently. In addition, this list of stages does not include the process of selling the bonds to investors that takes place from the formation of the syndicate to signing the subscription agreement.

Mandate to the Lead Bank

The investment bank chosen to act as lead manager will discuss plans for the issue, and will agree on the broad terms, such as the amount of the issue, the currency of denomination, the form and status of the bonds and the probable issue price (interest rate). They also will discuss how the bonds should be marketed and sold, for example which countries should be targeted in particular for the selling. They will agree which bank should act as fiscal agent, or if there is to be a trustee, which organization should act as trustee and which bank should act as principal paying agent.

Having reached agreement on these matters and agreed the details, the issuer will give a mandate letter to the lead bank. This sets out the broad terms of the issue, and also authorizes the lead manager to announce the issue and to assemble a syndicate.

Due Diligence

Before the issue is launched and the syndicate is assembled, the lead manager will carry out due diligence. The due diligence process is a fact-finding exercise. The lead manager will be supporting and promoting the bond issue to other banks and to investors. It will have to be certain that the issuer's financial and commercial position is sound, that the information provided to other banks and investors is accurate and that no relevant information is overlooked or omitted.

Information must be gathered during the due diligence process for inclusion in the listing particulars if the bonds are to be listed, or into the offer document to potential investors if the bonds will not be listed.

The depth of the investigations in the due diligence process, and the checks that are carried out can vary considerably between different bond issues. The amount of due diligence needed will depend on:

- the closeness of the working relationship between the issuer and the lead manager in the past.
- whether the bond has made another bond issue recently, in which case much of the information obtained for that issue probably will be relevant to the new issue, and so already available.
- the time that has elapsed since the end of the company's most recent financial year, to which its most recently published audited accounts relate. The longer the time since the end of the most recent financial year, the more due diligence is required.
- the term to maturity of the eurobond. When bonds have a long term to maturity, investors will be exposed to the risk of default (the credit risk) for a longer time than with shorter-dated bond issues. Consequently checks and investigations will probably be even more careful.

Preparing the Documentation

Many of the documents, or large parts of them, are drawn up in standard form, using standard text provided by IPMA. Using standard documentation has the dual benefit of:

- speeding up the documentation process and
- reducing the possibility of disagreement or misunderstanding among the parties, because standard terms generally will be understood.

Roadshow

Bond issues are marketed to potential investors before the formal announcement and launch of the issue. The lead manager organizes a series of presentations by officers of the issuer to an invited audience of investment institutions.

The purpose of the presentations, referred to as a roadshow, is to market the issue by:

- creating an awareness of the forthcoming issue among potential investors
- creating a favorable impression of the issuer
- drawing attention to the main selling features of the bond.

The number of presentations that are made in a roadshow will depend on the size of the issue, the number of countries in which the bonds will be sold, and the whereabouts of the main financial centers in each country. A roadshow might involve a series of presentations in Frankfurt, Zurich, Geneva, Paris, Brussels, Dublin and London. The first presentation might take place about a week before the formal announcement and launch of the issue.

The early reaction to presentations in a roadshow will give the issuer and lead manager a good idea of the likely response of investors to the issue, and when the response seems hesitant or unfavorable, some of the terms of the issue might be amended.

Launch of the Issue and Forming the Syndicate

The bond issue is launched formally by public announcement. The launch date is agreed between the lead manager and the issuer, and will be after the completion of due diligence and the marketing presentations by the issuer.

An issue normally is announced to the market through electronic information such as Reuters that has a bookrunner page.

On the same day that the issue is launched, the lead manager sends an **invitation telex** to the banks invited to join the syndicate. Most often the lead manager will have put the syndicate together already because by sounding out the willingness of banks to become involved. The invitation telex is a formal process because the banks will have been invited informally and will have indicated in the same manner their willingness to join.

Once the banks have responded, the lead manager sends an *allotment telex* to each of them, stating the amount of bonds in the issue for which they will be asked to subscribe. Under IPMA rules, the allotment telex must be sent out within 24 hours of the launch of the issue.

If they have not started doing so already, the banks joining the syndicate will start to contact clients to sell the bonds, i.e. to obtain an indication of their willingness to purchase bonds. The banks will want to know the strength of investor interest in the bonds, and so whether they will be able to sell them, before they sign the subscription agreement. They will not want to subscribe for bonds that investors refuse to buy because this would leave them with unsold bonds on their books.

Listing the Bonds

The issuer may apply for the bonds to be listed. If so the lead manager is likely to act as listing agent for the issuer.

Gray Market

Before a bond issue is made, it is traded for a time in the gray market.

This is a market in which traders sell the bonds short. In other words, they sell bonds that they have not yet purchased because they have not yet been issued. Traders in this market hope to profit by purchasing the bonds after issue at a price lower than the price at which they have made their bond sales in the gray market.

A useful function of the gray market is that it gives the lead manager a good insight into what the market thinks the bonds are worth. A final decision about the issue price for the bonds can be delayed until a gray-market price becomes apparent.

Closing

Closing is the time when:

- the bond comes into existence, thereby creating the issuer's debt obligations
- the bond is placed with the depository, for safekeeping
- the syndicate banks obtain their allotment of the bonds and pay for them
- the money is paid, through the common depository, to the issuer.

Delivery versus Payment

Closing involves issuing the bonds to subscribers and obtaining payment for them, a process sometimes referred to as the closing mechanics. Delivery of the bonds should occur simultaneously with the payment, i.e. there must be delivery versus payment or DVP.

Preparations for settlement by DVP should be made in advance, between the signing meeting and the date of the closing meeting, and are orchestrated by the lead manager.

Before closing date, the lead manager will arrange with clearing systems Euroclear and Clearstream for the bonds to be accepted by the systems, and to be recorded in the lead manager's new issues account. The lead manager also will inform each of the systems what quantity of bonds will be allotted to the syndicate members who are participants (account holders) in their system.

Each syndicate member must instruct its clearing system to arrange for payment to be made for its bonds from its cash account in the system. The payment should be made to the new issues account of the lead manager, against delivery of the bonds into their securities clearance account with the clearing system.

The arrangements involve issuing instructions in advance to be carried out simultaneously on a specified date, i.e. as soon as closing occurs.

At closing, the money from the syndicate members is in place, ready for payment against delivery of the bonds. In addition, the clearing systems are ready to adjust the securities clearance accounts and cash accounts of its participants (account holders) who are members of the syndicate for the issue.

Stabilization

Stabilization is a price-supporting process, in which a dealer, a stabilizing manager, often the lead manager or co-manager for an issue, tries to maintain price stability for bonds in the after-market following the issue. The purpose of price stabilization is to effect an orderly distribution for the issue.

The intention to provide price stabilization must be notified in each advertisement for the issue and potential investors should be aware of it.

The main purpose of price stabilization is to prevent a large fall in the market price of the bonds. To sustain the price, the stabilization manager will be prepared to buy the bonds itself.

Price stabilization activity can be only temporary. Typically, the process has no fixed time period and can be discontinued at any time. It is unusual for price stabilization to last for more than 24 hours after the issue has been made.

Credit Ratings

The lead managing bank will insist on a credit rating for a eurobond issue. Credit rating is a key factor in the decision by investors to purchase bonds. Investors often establish internal guidelines for investment. For example, an investment institution could adopt a policy of never investing in an issue with a credit rating below investment grade or in an issue with no credit rating at all.

In addition, the yield expected by investors will depend on the bond's credit rating; higher yields could be demanded for bonds with lower ratings.

Credit ratings are described in Chapter 8.

Survey of the Bond Markets

The Eurobond Market

Eurobonds are issued outside the confines of the domestic bond markets, and the eurobond markets are relatively free from government regulation.

The eurobond market, like the eurocurrency market for bank lending in foreign currencies, came into being because of government regulations and restrictions in domestic markets. From 1963, the US government employed measures such as the Interest Equalization Tax that was not lifted until 1974, to discourage foreign borrowers from issuing bonds in US capital markets. The requirement for funds from large international borrowers was already high and no domestic capital market in any country outside the US could meet this demand on its own.

The eurobond market became a free and accessible capital market for international borrowers to raise long-term debt capital in sizable amounts.

There is now a large degree of deregulation in domestic bond markets, and foreign issuers now have much better access to the large and liquid domestic US bond market. However, the eurobond market has survived these changes because of the systems that have been established by the market.

- Bond issues can be offered to an international investment community enabling issuers to raise large sums of money
- Investors have a wider choice of where to invest their money
- The market has developed its own self-regulation, and can

reassure investors that their interests will be protected
- The market has fitted in with domestic market institutions, particularly in London.

The international market is still used more than most domestic bond markets for corporate bond issues.

Maturities and Currencies of Denomination

Eurobonds typically are issued with a maturity of between five and ten years, and the market is much less liquid for maturities beyond about five years. Some bonds are convertible, giving their holders the option to convert the bonds at a future date into equity shares of the issuer, at a specified rate of conversion. Some issues are made with equity warrants attached. The warrants are detachable from the bonds and are traded separately. They give the holder the right to purchase a quantity of new equity shares of the issuer at a future date and at a specified price.

Bonds might be denominated in any freely traded currency. Dollar-denominated bonds are the most common, and euro-denominated bonds have been common since the launch of the euro in January 1999. There are also periods of market interest in bonds denominated in other currencies such as the yen, sterling or Canadian dollar.

Bond issuers might decide to denominate the bonds in a currency that will attract investors, and arrange a currency swap to exchange their payment obligations in the currency of the bond for a currency of their preference. For example, a UK company might issue dollar-denominated bonds, and arrange a currency swap to exchange their dollar payment obligations for payment obligations in sterling.

Participants in the Market

The eurobond market, like any other capital market, consists of issuers, intermediaries and investors. Issuers are governments, supranational organizations, banks and large corporates. Investors are mainly large institutional investors in several countries, although there are significant numbers of private individual investors.

The market is operated and regulated by its intermediaries. Its self-regulatory association of members is the International Securities Association (ISMA), formerly called the Association of International Bond Dealers (AIBD).

A primary issue in the eurobond market takes place in several international centers simultaneously. Although the market is relatively free from government interference, permission from the national authorities could be required before an issue is made in a particular country.

Secondary-market trading is over-the-counter, investors buying and selling through dealers in any of several countries.

International Securities Market Association

ISMA is a self-regulatory body based in Zurich whose members, from about 40 countries, consist of the firms that deal in the international securities markets. It provides a regulatory framework for the international markets, and has established uniform practises that govern nearly all transactions in eurobonds between members. These practises also have extended to cross-border transactions in domestic bonds.

ISMA also has:

- introduced a standard method of calculating yields for eurobonds
- contributed towards the harmonization of procedures for settling market transactions, and cooperation between the two main settlement systems, Euroclear and Clearstream
- provided recommendations to issuing houses on the format of international securities and new-issue specifications.

ISMA also operates TRAX, an electronic system for matching and reporting transactions in the secondary bond market.

Dealers in the international markets must cooperate with national governments and ensure that market practise is consistent with national laws. ISMA provides a point of contact between the markets and government bodies.

International Primary Market Association

IPMA is a trade association of the leading underwriters in the primary international capital markets. Like ISMA, it is a self-regulatory association that has issued practise guidelines known as the IPMA Recommendations that it expects its members to follow. Its specific interest is with new issues, the cooperation between underwriters in a syndicate and standardized documentation. Members of IPMA are required to belong to ISMA, and there is a good working relationship between the two bodies.

The IPMA Recommendations are applicable to new issues and relate to matters such as:

- early disclosure of the terms of an issue
- underwriting commitments
- allotments of securities with investors
- payment of commissions
- stabilization
- delivery of bond/share certificates
- fixed-price offerings and reoffer schemes.

The Secondary Market in Eurobonds

Most eurobonds are tradable. Transfer of ownership normally is by physical delivery because most eurobonds are bearer bonds. Investors sell and purchase bonds in the secondary market through over-the-counter transactions with a dealer such as a securities house. Dealers usually do not take positions, i.e. buy and sell bonds on their own account to make a market. Instead, they try to bring sellers together with buyers to arrange matched bargain transactions. In the case of a liquid issue, however, a large number of market makers will be prepared to quote bid and offer prices at any time, and investors can sell or buy these bonds readily at a fair price.

Trades are agreed by phone, although moves towards electronic trading systems have begun. Once a trade has been made, each party to the transaction must confirm the transaction by matching the details. ISMA operates TRAX, an electronic system for trade matching in every type of international equity and debt security. Each party to a transaction inputs the transaction details into TRAX that matches them. TRAX also has a link to Euroclear and Clearstream, and transmits the trade details to them. Clearstream and Euroclear use the data as the basis for the settlement instructions for the trade. The data transfer from TRAX obviates the need to key in the data again for sending settlement instructions by the parties to the trade.

TRAX also allows subscribers to comply with the trade reporting requirements of the relevant government authorities or stock exchange by sending the information to the appropriate body automatically.

Liquidity

Liquidity in the eurobond market varies over time and between bond issues according to:

- the size of the issue
- the strength of investor demand for the bonds
- the willingness of existing investors to sell, and
- the commitment of dealers to each particular issue.

Some eurobonds do not have a liquid market. In particular, the high-yield bond market in Europe has been very illiquid, investors preferring to acquire high-yielding bonds as a long-term investment and for the benefit of the high-interest payments.

The market also is characterized by feast and famine, particularly in currencies other than the dollar and the euro. At times there are numerous new issues and trading activity is high. At other times, investor interest is low.

Eurobond Listings

There are no requirements for Eurobonds to be listed on an exchange. Most eurobond issues are listed and traded on the London or Luxembourg exchanges and so must then comply with the official listing regulations and the rules of the relevant exchange. Bond prices are quoted through the exchange's price-quotation system.

The reason for listing eurobonds is often technical. Managers in some investment institutions are permitted to invest only in listed securities. An exchange listing for eurobonds allows these institutions to invest in the issue.

Secondary-market trading in the bonds is transacted over-the-counter, through bond dealers, using ISMA procedures rather than the procedures of the exchange on which the bonds are listed.

Making Transactions

Trading in eurobonds is over-the-counter between investors or their brokers, and dealers. When a transaction is agreed at a clean price both sides must report the details to a central organization for confirmation. The buy and sell sides of the deal must match each other. Any discrepancies must be resolved immediately.

Confirmation

Confirmation is the process whereby the two parties to a bond transaction, having made the transaction, check to make sure that they agree the details. At one time, confirmation systems were paper-based but after ISMA introduced TRAX, a real-time computerized confirmation system that also provides a price-reporting system, ISMA has been able to provide up-to-date price information to market participants.

Settlement: Clearstream and Euroclear

The major clearing systems for eurobonds are Euroclear and Clearstream, and nearly all eurobond transactions outside the US are settled through one of these organizations.

In the Euroclear and Clearstream systems, bonds are placed in the custody of the system via a Europe-wide network of depository banks. In this way the physical transfer of bonds on settlement can be achieved by means of a computer transaction (a book entry).

Participants in Euroclear and Clearstream must be institutions, each having an account with the clearing system. Settlement – securities transferred against payment – can take place through the simultaneous exchange of bonds for cash on the books of the system.

An electronic bridge between the two systems allows transfers of securities from one system to the other.

International Bonds and Domestic Bond Markets

With some notable exceptions, in particular the US, the eurobond market offers a better source of capital for large corporate issuers than domestic bond markets and so is often preferred to domestic bond issues.

As capital markets have become more global, links are developing between domestic markets and international markets, and are likely to become stronger. Euroclear and Clearstream, for example, clear transactions in foreign bonds and domestic bonds, as well as in eurobonds.

Domestic bond markets can be an alternative to the eurobond market as a source of funding for companies. A company can issue:

- domestic bonds in its own domestic bond market, or
- foreign bonds in the domestic bond market of another country.

The differences between eurobonds and foreign bonds are:

	Foreign bonds	**Eurobonds**
Issued by	a foreign borrower	a borrower
In	a national capital market	an international bond market
With underwriting from	a syndicate of banks in that country	an international banking syndicate
Denominated in	the domestic currency of that country	any major currency
Regulation	subject to the securities laws of that country	not subject to the laws of any single country

The method of issuing bonds in a domestic market is similar to that for issuing equity shares. The choice between a public offering and a private placement as the method of issue will be determined by stock-market regulations. Secondary-market transactions in corporate bonds are similar to transactions in equities for price quotations, trading, confirmation and settlement procedures.

Disadvantages of Domestic Bond Markets

There can be several disadvantages to using the domestic bond markets for issuing corporate bonds. These include:

- regulation. Domestic bond markets operate within a national system of regulation and might be subject to more regulation than the eurobond market. The system of regulation varies from country to country
- the influence of government bond issues on corporate bond issues. In some countries, such as the UK, the domestic bond markets are dominated by government securities. This makes it difficult or expensive for corporates to issue bonds because corporate bonds represent a higher credit risk and investment risk for investors
- lack of investor interest in domestic bonds or poor liquidity in the secondary market.

There are some exceptions, and in some countries there is a large and liquid domestic bond market

US Bond Markets

The largest domestic bond market is in the US that can be an important source of capital for corporate borrowers. Some companies seeking to raise a large amount of capital through bond issues have made an international bond issue in Europe and the far east, and in addition have made another bond issue in the US domestic market.

Multinational companies with large US subsidiaries can use the subsidiary to issue bonds on one of the US stock markets, notably the New York Stock Exchange. Large foreign companies also can issue dollar bonds on the New York Stock Exchange. These are known as Yankee bonds.

Rule 144A

After the Wall Street Crash in 1929, the US government introduced several laws to protect investors, including the Securities Act of 1933 and the Banking Act of 1933 known as the Glass-Steagall Act.

The Securities Act requires a detailed registration to be filed for any security offered to the public. A condition of registration is the preparation of a prospectus for the issue that must be made available to all potential investors. The prospectus must include information about the nature of the issuer's business and the reasons for the issue, together with detailed financial information about the issuer. Registration is a lengthy, laborious and costly process.

There were some exemptions to the rules about registration. Section 144 of the act allows the issue and resale of unregistered securities, in cases where buyers would be investors with expertise in the markets and large capital resources, usually institutional investors.

In 1990, this part of the act was modified, making it easier to sell unregistered (restricted) securities. The modifications are known as Rule 144A. An issuer can sell unregistered debt or equity securities and avoid the difficulties and delays of registration. Although issues under Rule 144A are sometimes referred to as private placements there is no restriction on the numbers of investors who can buy the securities for any issue.

There are several conditions attached to issues under Rule 144A.

- Securities issued must not be of the same class as securities listed on a US stock exchange – they cannot be fungible with US-registered securities, but can be listed and traded on a foreign non-US stock exchange.
- The seller must take reasonable steps to ensure that a buyer is aware of the exemption from registration, and is a qualified institutional buyer (Qib).
- Buyers may ask for financial information about the issuer that the issuer must provide. The volume and detail of this information would be much less than for the prospectus for a registered issue.

A further modification introduced by Rule 144A is that buyers of restricted securities are no longer required to hold them for at least two years before they can be resold to a US investor. This relaxation of the rules about resale was intended to encourage a liquid secondary market in unregistered securities. But to attract investors it would be necessary for the securities to have either an investment-grade credit rating or to be actively traded on a recognized foreign non-US exchange.

The 144A market offers a low-cost method of raising funds in the US, and a potentially liquid market. NASDAQ, the computer-based stock exchange, has established a market for 144A issues of equities, bonds, notes, convertibles and other securities covering the primary issue, secondary-market trading, confirmation, clearance and settlement.

Regulation S

When Rule 144A was adopted in 1990, the SEC also adopted Regulation S. This exempts offers and sales of securities outside the US from registration under the requirements of the Securities Act of 1933. This assists US issuers of eurobonds or global debt.

Thus, while Rule 144A allows the resale of securities to Qibs within the US, Regulation S allows their resale outside the US.

UK Bond Market

The UK bond market is dominated by gilts – UK government bonds – and corporate bond issues are rare. When they are issued, UK domestic bonds can be in several forms including:

- debenture stock secured by a fixed charge
- debenture stock secured by a floating charge, and
- unsecured loan stock.

All bond issues are supported by covenants.

Maturities for corporate sterling bonds can be very long because there is demand from institutional investors for long-dated domestic-market issues. Sterling bonds with shorter maturities of up to ten years are more likely to be euro-sterling issues rather than issues in the domestic market.

Bond issues by foreign issuers on the domestic sterling market are called bulldog bonds. These are similar in many respects to sterling eurobonds (eurosterling bonds) and tap a similar investor base in the UK.

German Bond Markets

The domestic market in Germany is dominated by government bonds termed Bunds, and bonds issued by domestic banks. The non-bank corporate bond market is small.

Japanese Bond Markets

The Japanese bond market is large and has several categories of bonds including:

- government bonds
- municipal or local government bonds
- government agency bonds
- corporate bonds, and
- samurai bonds.

Samurai bonds are yen-denominated bonds issued in Japan by foreign issuers. Samurai bond issuers are supranational organizations, foreign governments and large multinational companies. Companies wishing to issue yen-denominated bonds are more likely to use the euroyen market than issue samurai bonds because regulations in the euroyen market are less restrictive.

Swiss Bond Market

Companies wishing to issue bonds denominated in Swiss francs must use the domestic Swiss bond market because government regulations forbid the issue of Swiss franc bonds outside Switzerland, making the foreign bond market in Switzerland quite large.

Medium-Term Notes (MTNs)

Medium-term notes are debt securities ranging in maturity from nine months, above 270 days in the US, to 30 years. The issuer promises to pay the noteholder a specified sum at maturity. Notes can be issued either as bearer securities or registered securities. The main MTN market is US-based, but a euro-MTN market also has developed.

MTN Program

Issues of MTNs are arranged within a program. A continuous MTN program is established with a specified issue limit. The size of an MTN program can be from as little as $100 million to $1,000 million or more. Within the program, MTNs can be issued at any time, daily if required although new issues are less frequent.

An MTN program is similar to a revolving loan facility. As maturing notes are redeemed, new notes can be issued. Usually the issuer can specify the maturity of each note issue within a program but the issuer cannot exceed the maximum limit of the program at any time.

Example
Alpha establishes a five-year $200-million MTN program and immediately issues the following notes:

- $50 million of notes with a one-year maturity
- $70 million of notes with a five-year maturity.

Analysis
Alpha can still issue a further $80 million of notes ($200 million – $50 million – $70 million). In one year's time when $50 million of notes mature, Alpha will be able to issue a further $50 million if required. The total amount of notes in issue at any time cannot exceed $200 million.

MTNs and Commercial Paper

MTNs are similar in some respects to commercial paper that is described in Chapter 8. Both MTNs and CP are securitized debt issued within a program and sold to investors mainly through dealers. However, MTNs differ from commercial paper in that they:

- have a longer maturity, and
- pay interest at a coupon rate, whereas CP usually pays no interest and is issued at a discount to face value.

Origins of the MTN Markets

The MTN market originated in the US. Some issuers sold notes to investors in the 1970s, for example GMAC, the General Motors Acceptance Corporation, but the market did not grow significantly until the early 1980s. Three important developments were:

- shelf registration
- credit ratings for proposed issues, and
- the creation of a liquid secondary market in MTNs in the US (US MTNs).

Shelf Registration
Shelf registration offers a facility for issuing debt securities quickly and easily. It is an off-the-shelf facility that can be prepared in advance in readiness for when an organization needs to raise capital. A shelf

registration allows an issuer to issue new securities within just a few days, even hours, taking advantage perhaps of a temporarily favorable window of opportunity in the markets.

Under US regulations, any corporate debt issued with a maturity of more than 270 days must be registered with the SEC. In 1982, the SEC adopted Rule 415 that permitted shelf registration of new corporate debt issues. A continuous MTN program can be registered in this way. All that a would-be issuer has to file with the SEC is:

- historical and current financial information, and
- the type and amount of securities it plans to issue under the program.

This is known as filing a shelf. The significance of Rule 415 and shelf registration for MTNs was that the administration of continuously offered notes became much easier for the issuer.

Before Rule 415, whenever an issuer published new financial results, or experienced a material change in condition, it had to rewrite and reprint all the issue documentation for submission to the SEC, and a new prospectus had to be produced every time a company wished to make an issue. Following the introduction of Rule 415 and shelf registration, updated information about the issue can be submitted simply by reference to the original filing, saving the issuer much time, trouble and expense.

An issuer, having filed a shelf for an MTN issue, can decide when to make an issue of notes. It does not have to issue the full amount for which it has filed nor does all the issue have be made at the same time. The issuer can choose the timing of each issue.

An issuer can announce interest rates for different note maturities, and sell notes with different maturities off the shelf through a dealer or group of dealers at its quoted rates. In this way MTNs provide the issuer with a means of raising funds continuously in different maturities.

In the US, shelf registration for debt securities is available to investment-grade foreign companies that have filed reports with the SEC for the preceding three years.

With an MTN program on the shelf a borrower has some control over debt issues that can be arranged to match its requirements perfectly. Issues of notes under a single MTN program can range from simple plain-vanilla instruments, i.e. fixed-rate term debt, to highly complex structured transactions.

Shelf registration is becoming available in other countries. It was introduced into the UK in May 2000, and other European countries are expected to follow this example. These developments could give a boost to regular debt-issuance programs in Europe, including MTN programs.

Credit Rating of MTN Issues

MTNs are unsecured. It is usual for a would-be issuer of US MTNs to seek a credit rating for the issue from a rating agency such as Moody's or Standard & Poor's, when it files the shelf registration. The rating is given by the agency for a specific amount of possible new debt. Should the issuer decide subsequently that it wants to increase the total amount of MTNs that could be issued, it will have to amend the shelf registration and also seek a review of the credit rating.

Rated MTNs should have an investment grade rating at issue because many investors will not buy notes with a junk rating below investment grade.

Liquidity of the Secondary MTN Market

A liquid secondary market in MTNs was first established in the US by Merrill Lynch that undertook to quote bid prices to any investor wishing to sell MTNs before maturity, provided that investor had bought the notes originally through Merrill Lynch. In other words, if an issuer of MTNs sold a new issue with Merrill Lynch as the dealer, Merrill undertook to create a liquid secondary market in the notes by acting as a willing purchaser. The success of the market resulted in more issuers, more investors and more firms willing to act as dealers. The US MTN market is now both large and liquid.

Even so, MTNs are not actively traded and dealers do not quote real-time prices on dealing screens. The market is liquid because dealers always are willing to buy from an investor. The comparative infrequency of trades stems from a disinclination of investors to sell, rather than from a lack of willing buyers in the market.

US MTNs

The US MTN market is the world's largest market for medium-term notes.

The main issuers of US MTNs are general finance companies, banks, US and non-US, governments and government agencies, supranational organizations such as the World Bank, US industrial and commercial companies, and thrifts in the form of savings and loan institutions.

There is large investor demand in the US for high-quality corporate paper, particularly with short-to-medium-term maturities. Because there is a large number of issuers and shelf registrations, investors can select issues that exactly meet their requirements for maturity and credit rating. The main US investors are investment companies, insurance companies, banks and bank trusts, thrifts, corporates and state institutions.

Bank Deposit Notes

Banks, both US and foreign, are big issuers in the US MTN market. Instead of issuing normal MTNs they issue fixed-rate bank deposit notes with maturities that usually are in the range of 18 months to five years.

Although bank deposit notes are similar in most respects to other MTNs, there are some differences. They originated in concept from the Certificate of Deposit (CD) and are securities backed by an underlying bank deposit. Under US regulations, bank deposits are exempt securities, therefore the bank does not have to register such note issues with the SEC.

The notes are secured through the Federal Deposit Insurance Corporation (FDIC). A bank issuing deposit notes pays an insurance premium of 8.125 basis points on all the notes it issues, and the FDIC insures investors against the first $100,000 of any loss they might suffer through failure of the bank to honor its payment obligations.

The success of bank deposit notes has been accompanied by a decline in the US CD market. The main advantage of bank deposit notes over CDs is their credit rating. Some US investors, particularly insurance companies, prefer to buy rated securities. Although the creditworthiness of banks is known because of the ratings for their other debt securities, CDs are not given any rating.

Bank Deposit Notes and Interest-Rate Swaps

For the issuing bank, deposit notes are a fixed-rate liability. Most assets of the banks, for example loans to customers, are floating-rate items, and banks normally will seek floating-rate funding to minimize the interest-rate risk. It is usual for banks that issue deposit notes to arrange interest-rate swaps, and swap their fixed-rate liabilities for floating-rate liabilities.

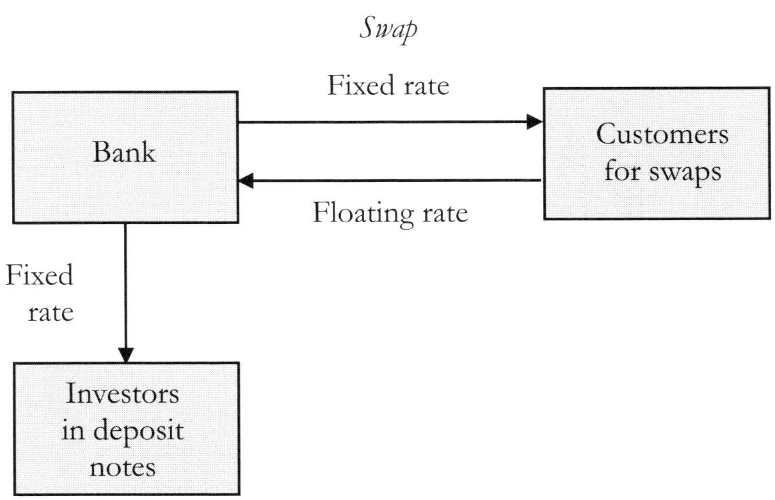

Some banks are able to reduce the net cost of their borrowing to below LIBOR by combining the issue of deposit notes with fixed/floating interest-rate swaps.

EMTNs

A euromarket in MTNs developed in the mid-1980s. Euro-MTNs or EMTNs, like eurobonds, are debt securities issued for distribution in several international financial centers.

Interest on most EMTNs is at a fixed rate. A program might be denominated in a single currency, such as the dollar but because it is expensive to establish a program, issuers may have a multicurrency option, or add a currency option into a program that already has been established. A large program could give a company the ability to issue in any of several different currencies within a single facility.

Maturities of EMTNs are mainly in the range of 18-36 months, although maturities of six years or longer are quite common.

Liquidity of Euro-MTNs
A problem with the international MTN market in the past has been its lack of liquidity that is a deterrent to investors.

Interest Rates on MTNs
The coupon interest rate payable on MTNs is different for each issue of notes within a program. The issuer decides what the coupon rate should be, and the price at which the notes should be sold. The coupon rate for an issue will be fixed with reference to yields on government securities – the yield curve – current market conditions and investor expectations.

Yields on fixed-rate MTNs in the US are quoted as a spread in basis points above comparable rates for Treasuries (US government securities). The size of the spread tends to widen when market interest rates are rising and to narrow when interest rates are falling. Spreads are narrower for issues with better credit ratings.

Only a small proportion of MTNs pay a floating rate, set at a margin above or below a benchmark interest rate such as LIBOR, the commercial paper index, the prime rate, the Treasury bill rate or the Federal funds composite rate. Reset intervals normally are weekly, monthly, quarterly or semi-annually.

Interest Payment Dates
Like bonds, interest on MTNs is paid on a 30/360-day basis, on the assumption of a year consisting of 12 months of 30 days each. Fixed-rate MTNs usually pay interest every six months. These dates are shown on the MTN certificate.

An issuer normally will pay interest on MTNs on two fixed dates in the year, regardless of when the notes were issued. Suppose, for example, that Alpha Inc pays interest on its MTNs on 15 May and 15 November each year. If it issues new MTNs on 1 April, the first interest payment on these notes will be on either 15 May or 15 November.

So although MTNs have differing maturity dates and coupon interest rates, they have standard interest payment dates and interest accrues on a common basis.

Arranging an MTN Issue

MTN issues, like eurobond issues are sold by a syndicate or group of dealer-banks. When establishing an MTN program, a prospective issuer should consider the appropriate size of the dealer group.

An MTN issuer in the US typically will use two to four dealers. For an EMTN program, five dealers might be appointed. Usually these would complement each other in terms of geographical spread. Other dealers outside the chosen syndicate could decide to trade in the issuer's notes. The issuer could try to restrict dealing in its MTNs to those dealers in its chosen syndicate. On the other hand, dealers outside the syndicate could be allowed access to the program, and when a new issue of notes is made, some could be made available, if required, to these dealers.

Underwriting
In the early years of the US market, MTNs were not underwritten. Dealers sold issues on behalf of the issuer on an agency basis, and took a fee, but did not guarantee to sell the notes. Some issues of MTNs and

bank deposit notes are now underwritten by the dealers who will expect a higher fee in return. Even so, many MTN issues are not underwritten, and this is one of the distinctive differences between long-term MTNs and corporate bonds.

Documentation for a Program

The issuer agrees with its dealers a common set of terms and conditions for any issues under the program, for example, warranties and representations, and events of default. Other terms specific to each issue of notes, such as price, interest-rate basis and maturity, are decided at the time of the issue.

The documentation must be sufficiently flexible to allow for notes to be issued in any form that might be required. The documentation could provide for:

- a wide range of currencies
- fixed and floating-rate issues
- a wide range of maturities
- coupon notes and zero coupon notes
- issues at par or at a discount
- notes with put or call options attached.

The documentation for a program takes about three months to complete and the cost of setting up a program can be up to $500,000.

Issuing Notes

The issuer posts rates with its dealers either daily or less frequently, and indicates the price it wishes to receive for an amount of notes of a given coupon and a specific maturity. The dealers will sell the notes to the market in the amounts wanted by the issuer. Trades will be confirmed with the issuer by each dealer who will take a fee, usually around 12.5 to 75 basis points of the amount issued.

In this way an issuer can have continuous access to the market, issuing new notes daily if required or at whatever intervals it chooses. MTNs ensure money is available for the issuer.

Reverse Enquiry
One method of arranging note issues is reverse enquiry. The initiative for issuing the notes comes from an investor rather than an issuer. An investor wanting to purchase notes or bonds to a particular specification, e.g. for a given maturity and in a given currency, can notify a dealer. The dealer then identifies a company with an MTN program that could be interested in issuing notes to the investor's specification. If a price for the notes is agreed, they are issued for purchase by the investor.

Book Entry MTNs
MTNs might be issued in certificate form. However, a paperless book-entry system has been in existence for MTN issues since the 1980s. The first was for Chrysler in 1988. A book-entry system records ownership and transfers by computer, and is cheaper than a paper-based system for clearing trades.

MTNs or Corporate Bonds?

A company wishing to raise a quantity of medium-term or long-term capital over a period of time must choose between issuing MTNs or long-term corporate bonds.

MTNs can be issued continually over time to match the funding requirements of the issuer. An MTN program should be preferred to a bond issue by a company that does not need all its funding at once, nor for the full duration of the program.

Corporate bonds should be preferred:

- by issuers that need all or most of the money immediately, or
- in the case of fixed-rate bonds, by issuers that expect interest rates to rise in the foreseeable future and therefore prefer to lock in a fixed-rate for all the funds by making a bond issue.

MTNs, as securitized debt, are also an alternative to medium-term bank facilities as a source of funds. Shelf registration and a liquid market can make MTNs more convenient for a company than borrowing from banks.

7

Commercial Paper (CP)

Commercial paper (CP) is a short-term unsecured promissory note. The issuer of the note promises to pay its holder a specified amount at a specified future date. CP normally has a zero coupon and is sold to investors at a discount to its face value. The discount represents interest to the investor in the period to maturity. Some CP is interest-bearing but this is less common. Any interest paid normally is free of withholding tax.

Example
Alpha Inc issues a CP note for $1 million on 1 April, promising to pay the holder this amount in six months' time, on 1 October. The CP is purchased by an investor for $960,000. If the investor holds the CP until maturity, there will be a profit of $40,000 ($1 million - $960,000). This is in effect the interest earned on an investment of $960,000 for six months.

All CP is negotiable, and can be resold in a secondary market before maturity. However, most CP is held by investors until maturity.

CP normally is issued in bearer form, and so ownership is anonymous although CP can be issued in registered form.

CP Markets

There are two major CP markets:

- the dollar CP market (USCP), and

- the eurocommercial paper (ECP) market that is much smaller.

The USCP market is the domestic US market for commercial paper, but it can be accessed by non-US corporations. ECP can be issued in any freely traded currency, including dollars.

Domestic markets in CP in Europe can exist, but are very small. In France, CP programs were first established in the 1980s and commercial paper is known as Billets de Trésorerie or BdT.

CP Programs

Although CP is a short-dated security, it is issued within a longer-term program, typically three to five years for eurocommercial paper. US commercial paper programs generally are open-ended, with no specific term. For example, a company might arrange a five-year CP program with a limit of $200 million. Once the program is established, the company could issue CP up to this amount, typically with maturities of 30 or 60 days. The program would be continuous, and new CP could be issued at any time, daily if required. CP matures continually and is repaid, so that more CP can be issued. The total amount of CP in issue at any time cannot exceed the limit for the program.

If the full $200 million is needed for several years, the company would issue CP at the start of the program perhaps with a maturity of six months. On maturity, the issue would be rolled over for a further six months by redeeming the maturing first issue with the proceeds of another CP issue. Issues can be rolled over in this way for the full term of the program if required.

The size of a program is measured by the limit on borrowing. The minimum program is between $100 and $150 million. Because CP is issued within a rolling program over several years, it can be regarded as a source of long-term funds for issuers, as well as a short-term money market instrument.

Continuous Offerings

Normally in CP markets issuers post offering levels each day, offering a quantity of new CP to the market in a price range agreed with the issuer's dealer. This continuous offering is a normal feature of a CP program.

Standby Line of Credit

Issuers of CP often roll over their funding and use funds from a new issue of CP to redeem a maturing issue. There is a risk that an issuer could be unable to roll over the paper because of a lack of investor interest in a new issue.

An issuer usually will provide protection against this risk by arranging a standby line of credit from a bank, preferably for 100% of the amount of the CP program, although highly rated issuers with a very large CP program could have a line of credit for as little as 60% of the value of the program. In an emergency, funds to pay off maturing paper can be obtained by drawing down the standby credit.

Investors could refuse to buy an issuer's CP unless an adequate standby line of credit is in place.

A standby credit line in support of a CP program can be:

- a standard line agreement
- a swing line, or
- a revolving line of credit.

A standard line agreement allows the borrower to activate the line of credit if required to do so. The drawn-down borrowing turns into a 90-day note and is repayable in full at the end of this time.

A swing line allows the borrower to draw down funds on one day and repay whenever it chooses within a maximum stipulated period of time. Swing lines are attractive to companies that experience a short-term and unanticipated need for cash because the drawn funds can be repaid quickly, thus minimizing the interest cost of using the credit.

Issuers of CP can back a portion of their program with a revolving line of credit. This is a line of credit that the bank agrees to keep in place up to a specified limit for a number of years. For example, if a customer borrows $30 million under a revolving line of credit for $50 million, and subsequently repays this borrowing, the unused line of credit will be restored to $50 million. A revolving line of credit in effect converts the portion of the CP program backed by the credit into the equivalent of a medium-term loan because the bank guarantees continual funding through the standby credit.

Borrowers pay a fee for a standby line of credit. A revolving credit also will incur an additional commitment fee of perhaps 25 basis points.

MTNs and CP Compared

Commercial paper and medium-term are issued within a program. However, there are key differences between these two types of paper.

- Most MTNs have a longer maturity.
- Most MTNs pay a coupon rate of interest, whereas most CP has a zero coupon and is issued at a discount to face value.
- The CP market is issuer-driven, with daily offerings to the market. The MTN market, in contrast, is more investor-driven. Issuers will offer MTNs to the market when demand appears – issues are often opportunistic, taking advantage of favorable conditions in the market.

USCP Market

The domestic US market is the world's largest CP market.

Maturities

USCP can be divided into two types:

- Section 3 (a) 3 paper. This is CP issued to finance current transactions. It does not have to be registered with the SEC. Its maturity can range from overnight up to a maximum of 270 days. Securities with longer maturities must be registered with the SEC before issue, but normally the maturity of most USCP is far shorter, typically about 30 days.
- Section 4 (2) paper. This is CP issued to finance acquisitions and fixed-asset purchases. It has no maximum maturity, but most often maturities are similar to those of Section 3 (a) 3 paper. Section 4 (2) paper must be privately placed on issue.

Credit Ratings for USCP

The issuer's promise to pay the CP at maturity is unsecured, and investors must rely on the creditworthiness of the issuer as an assurance of eventual payment. Almost all USCP is given a credit rating by one or more of leading US agencies Moody's and Standard & Poor's. A CP issue needs a high credit rating to attract investors and most CP issued in the New York market has a rating of A1/P1 or even better. Credit ratings are explained in Chapter 8.

Interest Rates on USCP

Although CP is sold at a discount, it has an effective interest rate. USCP trades at a margin above dollar LIBOR, the international benchmark cost of short-term borrowed dollar funds.

USCP yields normally are much higher than yields on Treasury bills of similar maturity, to compensate investors for:

- the higher credit risk, and
- the lower liquidity in the USCP market compared with the bills market.

Issues with a higher credit rating should attract a lower rate of interest, i.e. a lower discount to face value, on issue. The yield difference might be about ten to 20 basis points (0.10% - 0.20%), possibly more, between CP rated A1/P1 and CP rated A2/P2.

Discount Rate

In the USCP market prices are quoted by dealers as a discount rate. This is the rate of discount to face value at which the CP is being issued or sold. At a 7% per annum discount rate, for example, CP with a maturity of one year would be issued at 93.00 (100 minus 7%). At a discount rate of 7% per annum, CP with a maturity of 180 days would be issued at 96.50 (100 minus [180/360 x 7.00]). The size of the discount to par value at which CP is sold reflects the interest rate that the buyer wishes to receive. The discount rate is not the same as the interest yield, however. This will be explained later.

The size of discount can be calculated from the formula:

$$D = \frac{F\,(d \times t)}{360}$$

Where

- D is the discount in dollars
- F is the face value of the CP
- d is the discount rate as a proportion, for example, 7.5% or 7½% = 0.075
- t is the term to maturity, in days

Example

A 60-day USCP note has a face value of $100,000. It is issued at a discount rate of 7.50% per annum.

Analysis

The discount is as follows:

$$D = \frac{\$100{,}000\,(0.075 \times 60)}{360} = \$1{,}250$$

The issue price for the $100,000 CP note is at a discount of $1,250 to face value, and is therefore $98,750 ($100,000 - $1,250).

Money Market Yield

The money market yield on USCP is the return to investors on the amount of their investment, expressed as an interest rate on a 360-day basis. The yield can be calculated from either of the following two formulae

$$\text{Yield} = \frac{360 \text{ x } d}{360 - (d \text{ x } t)} \text{ x } 100\%$$

or

$$\frac{D}{(F - D)} \text{ x } \frac{360}{t} \text{ x } 100\%$$

Example

Continuing the previous example, the money market yield on the CP at the time of issue was:

$$\frac{(360 \text{ x } 0.075)}{360 - (0.075 \text{ x } 60)} \text{ x } 100\% = 7.59\%$$

Another way of calculating this yield is to measure the capital gain, that is the discount, as a percentage of the CP's cost, and convert this from a 60-day yield to a one-year 360-day yield, as follows:

Yield =

$$\frac{1{,}250}{98{,}750} \text{ x } \frac{360}{60} \text{ x } 100\% = 7.59\%$$

Exercise

Try your own solution to the following problem. A company wishes to issue US commercial paper with 90 days to maturity. The investment bank that is managing the CP program advises the company that the discount rate should be 9.5%.

What should be the issue price of the CP? What would be the money market yield for investors?

Solution

The discount should be

$$\frac{100 \text{ } (0.095 \text{ x } 90)}{360} = 2.375$$

The issue price should be 97.625 (100 - 2.375). The yield to investors will be:

$$\frac{2.375}{97.625} \times \frac{360}{90} \times 100\% = 9.73\%$$

Who Issues and Who Invests in USCP?

CP is issued by many US companies, including banks and other finance companies, and significant numbers of foreign issuers including governments and government agencies, non-US banks and other companies, mainly European. Some foreign issuers use the USCP market to obtain dollar funding; others swap the dollars into another currency.

The main investors in USCP are investment companies, insurance companies, banks, commercial and industrial companies, and state and municipal funds

USCP Dealers

CP can be issued directly by the issuer to investors, or sold through dealers. The USCP market is dominated by a small number of dealers.

Dealers charge a fee to the client. The fee is charged on buying and selling the paper. It can be 5 basis points or less for large issuers, and perhaps 10 basis points for small programs. A fee of 10 basis points for issuing $100 million of CP would cost the issuer $100,000.

Dealers serve several valuable functions.

- Being close to the market, dealers can identify easily investors wanting to buy CP because they maintain regular contact with investors.
- There have been very few defaults in the USCP market partly

because dealers monitor closely the credit position of their clients and help to reassure investors.

- They can create a liquid market in an issuer's CP.

Arranging a Program

The most common method of issuing CP is through a dealer program. The company planning a CP program will be advised by an investment bank that normally will be named as the arranger for the program.

The arranger:

- establishes a dealer network subject to the issuer's approval, by inviting one or more other firms to act as dealers for the program. The number of invited dealers will vary with the size of the program
- appoints a paying agent that will be responsible for issuing and authenticating CP notes and for repayment of the principal at maturity
- advises on the documentation, regulatory requirements, legal aspects, timing and pricing for the issue.

A credit rating must be obtained before a dealership network can be established.

Issuing CP

The issuer decides when it wants to issue CP, for what maturity and in what amounts. The issuer also can decide what price it wants for the issue, but its arranger will expect to offer advice on price. Most issuers give their dealers discretion each day to trade within a certain interest-rate band to allow for fluctuations in market rates during the day. The dealer will post details for the CP that the issuer wants to sell, including amount, maturity and discount rate. The sales team then tries to sell the issue to investors.

Arranging a CP Program

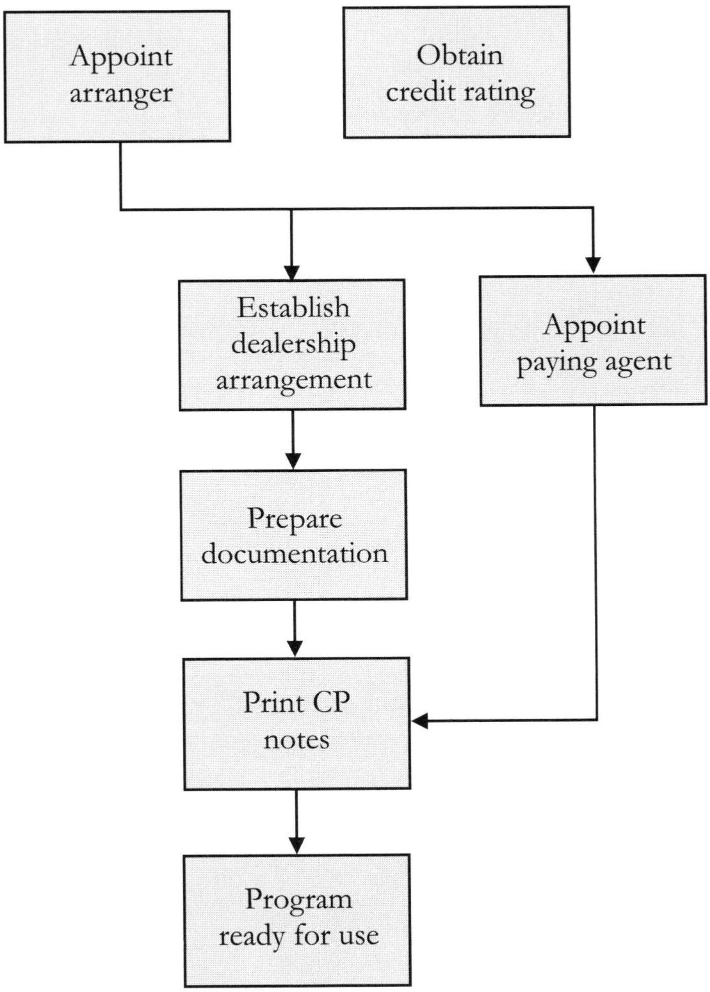

A typical schedule for selling CP:

Early morning	Issuer notifies the dealer of its intention to issue CP that day, specifying the amount, maturity and preferred price. The dealer and issuer agree the plan.
Morning	The dealer sells the CP to investors. Details of trades are confirmed with the issuing and paying agent.

Early afternoon	The issuing and paying agent authenticates notes for issue and ● credits the dealer's account with the notes ● debits the dealer's account with the funds payable.
Mid-afternoon	The dealer delivers the CP to the investor against payment in Federal Funds. The dealer then wires Federal Funds to the issuing and paying agent.

Secondary Market in USCP

Dealers provide a secondary market for USCP, and are willing to buy back from investors paper that originally was sold through them. The bid-offer spread, the difference between the interest rate at which a dealer will buy back CP and the rate at which the dealer will sell it, depends on market conditions. In the USCP market, the bid-offer spread typically is just 5 basis points (0.05% or 0.0005).

Types of USCP

USCP issued through dealers to the investing public, that is any wholesale investor, is known as plain-vanilla CP.

LOC commercial paper is USCP backed by a confirmed and irrevocable letter of credit from a top-rated bank. This is a guarantee from the bank that it will pay all amounts owed to CP investors should the issuer fail to do so. Rating agencies will rate LOC commercial paper on the creditworthiness of the bank, not the issuer.

The purpose of LOC commercial paper is to obtain a better credit rating for the CP than the issuer could obtain, thereby improving the attractiveness of the issue to investors and, in all probability, a lower discount rate for the paper.

Direct Issue CP

Some US issuers of CP, mainly large finance companies, issue CP directly to investors without using dealers as intermediaries. To place CP directly, the company will approach a regular group of investors whenever it wishes to issue paper, but also will post prices on an information system such as Reuters.

A feature of direct-issue CP is that the issuer will, at the request of the investor, prepay – redeem – issued paper before maturity using a specified pricing formula. Some issuers do this at no penalty, and prepay paper at the same interest rate at which the CP originally was issued.

The willingness of direct issuers to prepay is equivalent to the secondary market in other CP provided by dealers. However, a secondary market also is created by dealers in directly issued CP.

Eurocommercial Paper (ECP)

ECP developed in the 1980s as securitized debt became an alternative to syndicated bank lending as a method of raising capital. Banks were becoming less willing to lend because they were having to pay a higher rate for their own funds and lending was less profitable and by the end of the 1980s, some of the banks' major customers had a higher credit rating than many of the banks. Reduced profits on lending meant banks turned to alternative products on which they earned fees acting as intermediaries. Consequently there was a development in the markets for securitized debt instruments.

ECP evolved from the euronote market. A euronote is a short-term promissory note, issued under a syndicated medium-term facility. Euronote facilities were underwritten by a syndicate of banks, so that an issuer of euronotes could be certain that its notes would be purchased on issue.

Euronote facilities were called Revolving Underwriting Facilities (RUFs) or Note Issuance Facilities (NIFs).

- In a RUF, notes were distributed by a bank acting as sole

placing agent. The bank tried to sell notes to investors, and would call on the underwriters to purchase the notes only if other buyers could not be found.

- In an NIF arrangement, the sole placing agent was replaced by a tender panel of banks that put in competitive bids to purchase notes at an interest rate at or below the rate obtainable from the underwriting banks.

Eurocommercial paper, like a euronote, is a short-term bearer promissory note. However, unlike euronotes

- an ECP issue is not underwritten
- ECP also is offered continuously to the market, via dealers, with maturities to suit the issuer's cashflow requirements, or at maturities for which attractive interest rates are obtainable.

Maturities

Maturities of seven days to one year are permitted for ECP. Average maturities are about 90 days – longer than for USCP.

Currencies

Most ECP is denominated in dollars (eurodollars) but other currencies might be used.

Credit Ratings

ECP programs are given a credit rating. At one time, European issuers of CP often were reluctant to go to the expense and trouble of obtaining a credit rating for their programs. Investors accepted this, relying on name recognition and the credit rating of the issuer, rather than on a rating for the paper, but as with USCP issuers obtained the backing of a standby line of credit from a bank.

Credit rating has become a necessity, and investors in ECP and non-US domestic CP such as sterling CP, would expect a program to have a credit rating. This means that it is difficult for small companies to establish a CP program because their credit rating is unlikely to be sufficiently high.

In the ECP market, credit ratings became important for three main reasons

- the large number of issuers. When there is a large number of CP programs, investors cannot analyze the creditworthiness of every issuer
- a large proportion of foreign investors in a company's CP. Reputation carries less weight with foreign investors than with domestic investors
- occasional instances of default.

ECP Interest Rates

It is usual to quote ECP rates at a spread to interbank rates (LIBOR) because investors regard ECP as an alternative to investing in the interbank market. Interest rates vary according to the issuer, but might be somewhere between 25 basis points below LIBOR to 15 points above.

Price

The price of ECP depends on the yield to investors. ECP is priced on an actual/360-day basis as follows:

$$\text{Price} = \frac{\text{Nominal amount}}{\left[1 + \dfrac{(\text{Yield x Number of days})}{(100 \text{ x } 360^*)}\right]}$$

*365 in the case of sterling-denominated CP

Example

A $100,000 CP note with a 90-day maturity and yielding 8% would be issued at a price of:

$$\left[\frac{\$100{,}000}{1 + \dfrac{(8.00 \text{ x } 90)}{(100 \text{ x } 360)}}\right]$$

= $100,000/1.02 = $98,039.22

Exercise

Try to find your own solution to the following problem.

Two companies, Sierra and Tango, each issue $10 million of ECP with a 90-day maturity. Sierra's CP has an A1/P1 credit rating, and was issued at a yield of 6.6%. Tango's CP has a lower credit rating, and was issued at a yield of 7.8%.

What was the issue price for Sierra's CP and Tango's CP?

Solution

Sierra will sell its CP at the following price:

$$\left[\frac{\$10 \text{ million}}{1 + \frac{(6.60 \times 90)}{(100 \times 360)}}\right] = \frac{\$10 \text{ million}}{1.0165} = \$9{,}838{,}700 \text{ approx}$$

This represents an issue price for the CP of 98.39.
Tango will sell its CP for a lower price:

$$\left[\frac{\$10 \text{ million}}{1 + \frac{(7.80 \times 90)}{(100 \times 360)}}\right] = \frac{\$10 \text{ million}}{1.0195} = \$9{,}808{,}700 \text{ approx}$$

This represents a lower issue price for the CP, of 98.09. Investors in Tango's CP demand a higher yield to compensate them for the greater credit risk.

Who Issues and Who Invests in ECP?

Issuers of ECP could be banks or non-bank corporates. Occasionally, sovereign issuers and government agencies also have had ECP programs.

Investors in ECP are mainly non-US institutional investors, banks and other companies.

ECP is not sold to US-based investors because:

- US companies with an ECP program often also have a USCP program
- there would be withholding tax problems for US investors in ECP
- the SEC restricts the sale of ECP within the US

However, foreign subsidiaries of US parent companies can (and do) invest in ECP.

Arranging an ECP Program

Arranging an ECP program is similar to arranging a USCP program. It is usual for issuers to use more than one dealer. For each new issuer of ECP, the dealers prepare a memorandum. The memorandum provides information about the issuer to would-be investors, and is distributed internationally. The documentation is fairly minimal and administering an ECP issue is relatively simple and cheap.

Dealing

The ECP market is global, and ECP is sold to investors in many countries. Prices are quoted not just in London but also in Hong Kong and Singapore, so that a 24-hour market is available. However, most trading activity occurs in the morning period of the European time zones.

Clearing and Settlement

The clearing system for ECP operates through three specialist clearing houses, Euroclear, Clearstream and First Chicago Clearing Center. ECP notes usually are held by one of these three clearing houses on behalf of the investor that can transfer ownership by means of a book-entry transfer because there is no requirement for the physical delivery of the notes.

Most ECP transactions are for settlement after two days. For example, if a transaction is agreed on Monday, funds for settlement must be available on Wednesday.

Domestic CP Markets in Europe

The largest domestic European markets for CP, or corporate treasury bills as they are known in some countries, are France, the Billets de Trésorie or BdT market, Germany, the UK, sterling CP or SCP market, and Sweden

The sterling CP market is both a domestic market and part of the eurocommercial paper market. Sterling CP and eurosterling CP are indistinguishable. All CP programs in sterling are regulated in the same way by UK authorities. Foreign companies are allowed to establish SCP programs.

The issuer of SCP is subject to certain restrictions.

- A UK corporate issuer, or its 100% parent company, must have a London Stock Exchange listing.
- The maturity of paper must be at least seven days and under one year.
- The CP must be guaranteed by the issuer's 100% parent or a recognized bank.

Using a CP Program

A CP program can be used by a company to manage its short-term liquidity, i.e. mainly for working capital needs. New paper can be issued whenever a need for cash arises, and for an appropriate maturity.

A pattern for a typical CP program, with issues on most working days throughout the year, is illustrated below.

	Jan	Feb	Mar	Apr	May	Jun	Jul	Aug
Number of issues	27	29	25	25	33	4	44	17
Average issue ($ million)	13	11	15	10	16	14	18	20
Average maturity (days)	28	30	25	35	24	26	26	19
Monthly issue volume ($ million)	360	320	365	250	500	55	800	340
Outstanding at month end ($ million)	360	340	440	220	500	160	790	550
Outstandings as % of $1.5 billion program	24	23	29	15	33	11	53	37

8

Credit Ratings

A credit rating is a formal opinion, given by a rating agency, of the credit risk for investors in a particular issue of debt securities. Ratings are given to public issues of debt securities by any type of entity, including governments, banks and corporates. They are given to short-term debt including commercial paper, as well as bonds and notes.

Purpose of Credit Ratings

Investors in securities must accept the risk that the issuer will fail to pay interest or fail to repay the debt principal in full and on time. The credit risk is greater for securities with a long maturity. For example, if a company issues ten-year bonds, investors cannot be certain that the company will still exist in ten years' time. It could collapse and go into liquidation long before then. There is also some risk with short-dated debt securities, and there have been instances of default by issuers of commercial paper.

The prospectus or offer document for an issue gives investors some information about the issuer so that some credit analysis can be undertaken. Investors can study this information before deciding to invest. Credit assessments take up time and call for specialist skills of analysis. Large institutional investors could devote some resources to credit analysis, but it would be too costly to vet every issuer in every debt market.

Nevertheless the investor must make a decision about whether the credit risk with an investment is acceptable every time securities are purchased.

There are two common methods of assessing the credit risk:

- name recognition, and
- credit ratings.

Name recognition means the investor relies on the good name of the issuer, and accepts that the issuer is of such good financial standing that a default on interest and debt payments is most unlikely.

Credit ratings are a formal assessment for a given issue of debt securities of the likelihood that the interest and debt principal will be paid in full and on schedule.

How are Ratings Established?

Ratings are provided by specialist agencies. The major credit ratings agencies are Standard & Poor's, Moody's and Fitch. There are other ratings agencies in the US and elsewhere. It is usual for issues of bonds to be given ratings by at least two agencies.

On request, credit-ratings agencies will carry out a rating exercise on an issue of debt capital. The request for a rating comes from the organization planning the issue of bonds, notes or commercial paper program.

Although ratings are provided for the benefit of investors, the issuer bears the cost of the rating exercise, and the cost of having the rating regularly monitored after the issue has been made. It is in the issuer's interests to do this, because investors most often will refuse to subscribe to an issue unless a rating is provided.

Although the rating exercise involves a credit analysis of the issuer, the rating is applied to a specific debt issue. In other words, the credit rating is supplied not to an organization, but to its debt securities, and it is usual to refer to the creditworthiness of organizations in terms of the credit rating of their debt. A highly rated company might be referred to as a triple-A rated company.

Consequences of a Rerating

The rating for an issue is kept under review, and if the creditworthiness of the issuer improves or declines, the rating will be changed accordingly. The consequences of a downgrading of a credit rating will depend on the circumstances.

- The market price of the debt securities will fall, and investors will suffer a loss.
- If the issuer is planning to issue more debt securities, investors will demand a higher rate of interest to compensate them for the higher risk.
- In some cases, the issuer might have agreed to a condition whereby the interest payable on bonds or notes will be raised if their credit rating is downgraded to or below a certain level.

For example, a company issuing 6% bonds might agree to a condition that the coupon will be raised to 7% if the credit rating for the bond ceases to be investment grade and becomes speculative grade. A clause providing for a higher coupon in the event of a credit-rating downgrade is known as a step-up clause.

A further consequence of a downgrade in credit rating might be that the company's banks will want to review the terms of their variable rate loans to the company, and might be able to insist on a higher rate of interest.

Credit Watch

When doubts emerge about the creditworthiness of an issuer of debt securities, a credit-rating agency might announce that it is putting the rating under review, and that there is a possibility of a downgrade in the near future. This is referred to as being put on credit watch or rating watch.

When a debt issue is put on credit watch, the outcome might be an upgrading, a downgrading or a reaffirmation of the existing grading. A rating agency will indicate when a downgrading is under consideration by adding the words *with negative implications* to the rating that is under review.

What are the Ratings?

Credit ratings vary between agencies. Separate categories of ratings are given by each agency for:

- short-term debt that has an original maturity of 12 months or less
- long-term debt (bonds and notes).

It is also usual to distinguish between higher investment grade ratings where the credit risk is low, and the poorer speculative grade ratings where the risk is higher. Bonds with a speculative grade rating are known as junk bonds or high-yield bonds.

The ratings of Moody's and Standard & Poor's, the most commonly reported, are described below.

- S & P's ratings might be modified by a plus or minus sign to indicate the relative standing of the debt within each rating category. Plus indicates a higher grading and minus a lower grading. A rating of AA- will be lower than a rating of AA, for example, even though both ratings are in the same AA category.
- Moody's ratings have a suffix of 1, 2 or 3 for long-term debt, with 1 being better than 2, that is better than 3. For example, Moody's ratings A1, A2 and A3 are equivalent to S & P's ratings of A+, A and A-.

Moody's Short-Term Debt Ratings

Rating	Characteristics
Prime 1	Superior ability to repay. Assured sources of alternative liquidity. The issuer has a leading position in a strong industry. It achieves high returns on capital employed, and a high ratio of equity finance, i.e. financial gearing is low. It has a high level of profit cover for its interest charges (high interest cover), and has strong cash generation.
Prime 2	Strong ability to repay. Ample sources of alternative liquidity. Similar characteristics to Prime 1 rating, but to a

Rating	Characteristics (continued)
	lesser degree. More variability in the rate of profit growth, and in interest cover.
Prime 3	Acceptable ability to repay. Adequate sources of alternative liquidity. The issuer is more likely to be affected by changes in industry or market conditions. Variability in earnings could result in relatively high borrowing levels and a high level of leverage.
Not Prime	Short-term debt that does not fall into any of the other three categories. Below investment grade.

Prime 1, Prime 2 and Prime 3 are all investment grade ratings. Prime is often shortened to P. A top-rated short-term debt issue is graded P1.

Standard & Poor's Short-Term Debt Ratings

Rating	Characteristics
A-1	Highest category. Strong safety characteristics. An A-1 + rating indicates *extremely* strong safety characteristics.
A-2	Not as high as A-1, but the issuer still has a satisfactory capacity for timely payments.
A-3	Adequate capacity for timely payments, but more vulnerable to adverse changes in circumstances than debt rated A-1 or A-2.
B	Only speculative capacity for timely payment.
C	Doubtful capacity for payment.
D	Payment is in default.

The A-1, A-2 and A-3 grades are all investment grade ratings. Short-term debt issues given a top-grade credit rating by both Standard & Poor's and Moody's are referred to as A1/P1 debt.

Moody's Long-Term Debt Ratings

Rating	Characteristics
Aaa	Best-quality bonds. Gilt-edged. The debt principal is secure. Interest payments are very well protected by profits.
Aa	High-quality bonds, but quality not quite as high as Aaa bonds, possibly because of greater variability in the issuer's profit margins.
A	The bonds possess many favorable attributes and are medium-to-upper grade. Adequate security for principal and interest.
Baa	Medium-grade bonds, being neither highly protected nor poorly secured. The principal and interest payments are adequately secured at present, but some unreliability exists for the long term. Some speculative characteristics as investments.
Ba	Bonds that are judged to have speculative characteristics as investments. Usually only a moderate protection of principal and interest payments.
B	Bonds that generally lack the attributes of a desirable investment. Protection of principal and interest over a long period of time is not well assured.
Caa	Bonds of poor standing, with some threat to the security of principal or interest payments. Some such bonds might be in default already.
Ca	Bonds that are highly speculative as investments. Often in default.
C	Lowest rating. The bonds have very poor prospects of ever achieving an investment grade (non-speculative grade) rating.

Standard & Poor's Long-Term Debt Ratings

Rating	Characteristics
Investment grade	
AAA	Highest rating. Issuer has an extremely strong capacity to make interest payments and repayment of principal.
AA	Issuer has a strong capacity to make interest payments and repayment of principal. Only marginally weaker than AAA grade.
A	Also a strong capacity to make interest payments and repayment of principal, but with some susceptibility to adverse changes in circumstances and economic conditions.
BBB	Adequate capacity to make interest payments and repayment of principal, but this capacity could be weakened by adverse changes in circumstances. Not as secure as other investment grade ratings.
Speculative grade	
BB	Major continuing uncertainties or exposure to adverse changes in conditions could result in the issuer having inadequate capacity to make timely payments of interest and principal. This rating also is used for debt that is subordinated to senior debt with a BBB- rating.
B	The issuer currently is able to meet interest payments and principal repayments, but there is a greater vulnerability to default than with a BB rating. This rating also is used for debt that is subordinated to senior debt with a BB or BB- rating.
CCC	There is an identified vulnerability to default, and the issuer is depending on favorable economic, business and financial conditions to avoid default. This rating also is used for debt that is subordinated to senior debt with a B or B- rating.
CC	Debt that is subordinated to senior debt with a CCC rating.

Rating	Characteristics (continued)
C	Debt that is subordinated to senior debt with a CCC- rating. Also used for debt where a bankruptcy petition has been filed but the debt is still being serviced (interest payments are being made).
Other grades	
C1	Income bonds on which currently no interest is being paid.
D	Payment is in default, or a bankruptcy petition has been filed and default is likely.

Note: Subordinated debt is debt that will not be repaid in the event of liquidation of the company and its assets, until the senior debt has been repaid in full.

Summary

A credit rating will affect the interest rate at which organizations can issue new debt securities, or even whether they will be able to issue new debt securities at all. The purpose of a credit rating is to give investors a guide as to the likelihood of their receiving interest payments and repayment of the debt principal on schedule.

Investors can use credit ratings in several ways. They can:

- refuse to buy debt securities with a credit rating below investment grade, or below a particular investment grade rating
- expect a higher yield/return from securities with a lower rating
- sell securities from their investment portfolio whose credit rating is downgraded below a certain level.

Credit ratings are now essential in all major debt markets, with the exception of the domestic government bond markets.

US investors have been more willing to invest in junk bonds, and the high-yield bond market in Europe is less well developed than in the US.

Asset-Backed Securities

Asset securitization (asset-backed securities) is a form of capital market finance that is independent of the credit quality of the company seeking the finance. The identity of the company or companies seeking finance even can be hidden from investors, if anonymity is preferred.

Securitization is a process in which a pool of cash-generating assets is packaged together in order to create securities that can be marketed to investors. The assets are sold to a specially created company. The income generated by the assets is used, after paying management expenses, to pay interest or dividends to the holders of the securities in the form of bonds and shares in the company. The bonds and shares in the specially created company effectively are backed by the income-generating assets, and the credit standing of the company is as good as the creditworthiness of the assets that back it.

Asset securitization began in the US in the 1970s with mortgage-backed securities. Initially, these were mortgages packaged together and guaranteed by one of three government agencies:

- the Government National Mortgage Association or GNMA (Ginnie Maes)
- the Federal Home Loan Mortgage Corporation or FHLMC (Freddie Macs)
- the Federal National Mortgage Association or FNMA (Fannie Maes).

A package of mortgages might be sold to a specially created company, and securities in the company, mainly bonds, will be sold to investors. The buyers of the securities will receive their interest or dividend income from the company that will receive its own income from the interest payments and capital repayments of the individual mortgage holders. The mortgaged property also will provide asset security for the bondholders.

Conduit Vehicles (Special-Purpose Vehicles)

A typical method of establishing an asset-securitization program is for a financial intermediary to set up an off-balance-sheet organization, referred to as a special-purpose vehicle (SPV) or conduit vehicle.

This vehicle purchases cash-generating assets from a number of different corporate sellers, packages them, and issues asset-backed securities. The proceeds from the issue are used to pay the corporate seller of the assets.

Any security or guarantees attached to the assets are transferred from the seller of the assets to the SPV.

For the seller of the assets, the assets are sold without recourse. In other words, the seller receives an agreed price for its assets, but will not be expected to make up any shortfall should the level of non-payments exceed actuarial forecasts.

Arranging an Issue of Asset-Backed Securities

Asset securitization is arranged by a bank.

- A bank can discuss an arrangement with an individual company that has cash-generating assets it might wish to sell. However, the value of the company's cash-generating assets must be large enough to warrant a stand-alone deal.
- A bank can invite a number of companies to discuss a common deal to sell selected cash-generating assets.

- A bank might wish to sell some of its own assets, for example mortgage loans.

The bank will investigate the potential client's cash-generating assets, to decide whether they are suitable for securitization. The bank also will ask for information to assess the payments records of the client's debtors in order to predict the probable volume of bad debts.

An agreement is then reached for the sale of selected assets by the client company or the bank, to an SPV that is established for the purpose.

The SPV raises funds to purchase the assets by issuing securities. These can be shares, bonds or commercial paper. There could be at least two classes of shares or bonds.

- Most would be in a class that is entitled to regular payments of interest or dividends out of the cash income generated by the assets. This class of bondholders or shareholders would be entitled to payment ahead of the other class.
- A smaller proportion of the shares/bonds would be in a higher-risk class. These would carry an entitlement to all the remaining income from the assets after management charges to the SPV and interest/dividend payments to the other class of bondholders/shareholders.

Income from the assets is collected by the company that sold them to the SPV and is paid over to the SPV. The SPV in turn uses this income to pay its bondholders and shareholders.

Once the arrangement has been established, the company or bank selling its portfolio of debts to the SPV will have to report regularly, typically monthly, on cash receipts and the current value of the sold assets for which full payment has not yet been received.

When asset-backed securities are in the form of CP, the SPV can establish a continuous program of CP issues. New CP can be issued, backed by new cash-generating assets. A continuing cycle will then exist for:

- buying assets
- issuing CP to pay for them
- collecting the cash income from the assets, and
- redeeming the CP.

Example

Banque Beta, a French bank, set up a special-purpose vehicle, known in France as an FCC, to purchase a selection of personal loans on which investors pay interest monthly. The average return on the personal loans is 11% per annum. The FCC issues two types of share:

- B shares that represent 8% of the nominal value of the personal loans purchased. The B shareholders receive all the remaining cash flows after payments on the A shares and payment of management charges to the FCC.
- A shares that represent 92% of the nominal value of the personal loans purchased. The A shareholders receive monthly payments at a coupon rate of 7.5% per annum on the nominal value of loans outstanding plus any early repayments of loans received during the month.

The A shares are given a credit rating by Moody's and sold to investors.

Credit Risk and Asset-Backed Securities

A problem with securitization is the uncertainty, due to bad debts, of the eventual cash value of the assets. For example, if a bank wishes to sell securities backed by $200 million of mortgages, the value of the securities will depend on how many of the mortgage loans turn into bad debts. If the credit risk is high for the investor, no one will want to buy the securities, except at a low price.

There are three basic ways of dealing with the problem of credit risk.

- Assess the credit risk in the assets and sell the securities at a price that allows for the risk. For example, if the bad-debt risk from mortgages is thought to be 2%, mortgage-backed securities could be sold at a price of $98 per $100 of mortgages.

- Create two classes of securities, one ranking below the other in the right to receive income from the assets, this was referred to earlier. For example, suppose that a bank wishes to set up a special-purpose vehicle and securitize some of its mortgage-loan portfolio. For every $100 of loans, the special-purpose vehicle could issue $95 of loan stock and sell this to investors. Investors would receive interest at a specified rate on the stock. The SPV also could issue $5 in subordinated debt per $100 of mortgages that the bank would own. The holders of these bonds would be entitled to any residual proceeds after paying the loan stockholders and management fees/commission to the SPV.
- Obtain the guarantee of a third-party organization, typically a specialist financial insurer, for the securities. This should give the securities the same credit rating as the guarantor, i.e. it is a means of credit enhancement for the securities.

There is a requirement among US investors for asset-backed securities to be rated by at least one of the major credit-rating agencies. This could add about 4 or 5 basis points (0.04% to 0.05%) to the cost of a typical issue. Legal costs must be borne by the issuer and there is also the cost of credit enhancement, via a bank letter of credit or a specialist insurer's guarantee that can cost up to ten basis points per annum.

Choice of Assets for Securitization

The largest market for securitized debt in Europe is the mortgage-backed securities market although this is extremely small compared to the US mortgage-backed securities market. Nevertheless other income-generating assets can be used to provide backing to specially issued securities. These include bank loans, car loans and credit-card debts.

Issuers' and Investors' Risks

Issuers of debt securities use the bond and CP markets to raise capital. They should not only seek to obtain funds as cheaply as possible over the medium-to-long term, but also try to ensure that the markets always will be accessible, if they should need new finance or refinancing at any time in the future.

Issuer's Financial Risk and the Debt Markets

The financial risks for a company issuing debt securities are mainly:

- price risk
- contamination risk
- refinancing risk, and
- currency risk.

Price Risk

An issuer could fail to obtain the best price for an issue and so incur higher interest costs. Two reasons for this price risk are:

- timing of the issue, and
- caution.

The timing of issues can be very important. There could be a short window of opportunity during which favorable interest rates are obtainable in a particular debt market. If such an opportunity is missed, an issue will have to be made at a lower price. A cautious approach to pricing is to set the offer price on the low side to improve the chances of the issue being fully subscribed.

When an issue price is lower than it could have been, the bond's price should rise in secondary-market trading.

Example
Tango, a UK multinational, has established a flexible program for issuing medium-term notes. The program is managed on Tango's behalf by Silver Securities, a securities house.

Silver Securities informs Tango's corporate treasurer that a large investor wishes to put $10 million into five-year notes, and would be willing to accept an interest rate that is a few basis points below the rate that Tango might normally expect to pay.

Tango could have an opportunity to issue notes to the investor and raise five-year funds at an attractive rate. If it hesitates, the opportunity could be lost, and the investor could put the money into a different investment.

Contamination Risk
Contamination risk is the possibility that an unsuccessful issue by a company, or by another issuer in the same market could affect adversely the success of future issues by the company. Issuers should seek to avoid an issue failure, even if the issue is fully underwritten, and to keep out of a primary market in which investor dissatisfaction currently is quite high.

Example
Romeo plc, a UK company, is planning to raise funds in the UK commercial paper market although there has been a default recently by Zeta plc, another issuer of CP in the market.

The default on debt payments by Zeta could contaminate investor attitudes to Romeo's proposed commercial paper program because of the fear of default by another borrower in the market. If investors are unwilling to put money into Romeo's CP, Romeo will have to abort its planned program.

Refinancing Risk
There is a risk with any issue that the issuer might not be able to make interest and principal payments on schedule and so would be forced to seek refinancing. This risk faces both the issuer and investors. A company should seek to restrict refinancing risk by avoiding excessive financial gearing.

Currency Risk
There is a risk for an issuer of debt securities that the currency in which the securities are denominated could strengthen in value against other currencies. This could increase the company's cost of servicing and repaying the debt.

Example
Sierra plc, a UK multinational, raised $210 million from an issue of bonds. The bonds were at a fixed coupon of 6% per annum. The dollars were sold in exchange for sterling, and the funds were invested in the UK at an exchange rate of £1 = $1.50.

The dollar subsequently strengthens in value against sterling, to £1 = £1.40.

Analysis
The $210-million bond issue was sold for £140 million in sterling ($210 million ÷ $1.50 to £1). With the change in the exchange rate, and the stronger dollar, the cost of repaying the bonds will rise to £150 million ($210 million ÷ $1.40 to £1). Interest payments, if made from sterling income, also will be more costly than expected.

Risks for the Investor in the Debt Markets

Investors in bonds and CP can be exposed to significant risk. They can suffer losses from unfair or dishonest dealings by issuers of securities, intermediaries and other investors. The purpose of market regulation is to protect investors from such activities.

The risks for an investor include:

- credit risk
- currency risk
- market liquidity risk
- investment risk.

Credit risk varies between different issuers and also with the maturity of the debt securities and between different markets. Credit ratings, described in the previous chapter, can provide some protection against credit risk.

Currency risk can arise for investors in securities denominated in a foreign currency. If the currency falls in value against the investor's domestic currency, the market value of the investment in the investor's currency, will fall and the investor will suffer a loss.

Market liquidity risk arises from lack of liquidity in the secondary market. In a liquid market, investors can buy or sell their securities without difficulty at a fair price. When a market is illiquid, buying, and more significantly selling, is much more difficult. An investor wishing to sell securities but unable to find a ready buyer could either:

- hold on to the securities and hope that a buyer eventually will be found, or
- reduce the price below a fair value in order to attract a buyer, and consequently receive less for the securities than they ought to be worth.

Some bond markets are very liquid. Some go through periods of liquidity and illiquidity. Others are illiquid most of the time. A serious risk for bond investors could be that at the time of buying their investment, there was a liquid market that dried up and became illiquid. As a consequence, their investments will fall in value and be difficult to resell.

Investment Risk

Investment risk is the possibility that an investment will fall in value, and the investor will incur a loss. If the debt issuer is a company that goes into liquidation, the full investment could be at risk. More commonly, investments could lose value in the secondary market. Bonds whose prices are more volatile are potentially a greater investment risk than bonds whose prices tend to be more stable over time.

In Chapter 3 it was explained that the market value of debt securities will fall if current market rates of interest go up. It was also explained that the volatility of a bond's price depended partly on:

- the remaining term to maturity, and
- the coupon rate of interest.

The price volatility of bonds can be measured, possibly by measurements of duration and convexity, and an investor can select a bond portfolio that has an acceptable level of investment risk.

Conclusion

Issuers of debt securities have to appreciate the factors that influence investment decisions, and the risks for investors. Decisions about when to issue securities, in what form, at what coupon and for what maturity, should be influenced by the likely response of investors. This calls for an understanding in particular of:

- credit risk – how a credit rating could be helpful
- market liquidity risk – the choice of market for making an issue, and
- investment risk and price volatility – duration and convexity.

Index